Halo

The Story Behind Depeche Mode's Classic Album Violator

Kevin May and David McElroy

Grosvenor House
Publishing Limited

This book is published by
Grosvenor House Publishing Ltd
Link House
140 The Broadway, Tolworth, Surrey, KT6 7HT.
www.grosvenorhousepublishing.co.uk

A CIP record for this book
is available from the British Library

ISBN 978-1-80381-225-0

For Andy ‘Fletch’ Fletcher

Contents

Acknowledgements

From Kevin and David

Researching and writing (and everything else associated with publishing a book) about a band that many people know and love is a fairly daunting undertaking.

We have juggled the book with our jobs, accidents, COVID-19, ups and downs, highs and lows – in fact, there have probably enough things going on in our respective lives to give Martin Gore a few more albums worth of material to write about. Perhaps not quite as sexually charged as some of his writing can be…

And, of course, in 2017 and 2018, there was a lot of Depeche Mode activity by way of countless gigs that we saw between us, spanning seven countries and maybe the need to extend our respective mortgages.

From the outset, we wanted Dave Gahan, Martin Gore, Andy Fletcher and Alan Wilder to share their perspectives and recollections of the 'Violator' era with us.

Undeterred, when we inevitably received the dreaded rejection emails (as many authors have in the past), we instead decided to track down and talk to as many other people associated with this extraordinarily creative period in the life of the band.

Everyone who spoke to us, either on the phone, on video calls or via email, was wonderfully generous with their time and we are extremely grateful for the contributions, especially Steve Lyon, Gareth Jones and Bruce Kirkland who welcomed Kevin into their recording studios in London and office in Los Angeles respectively.

From Nils Tuxen (steel guitar player on 'Clean'), Richard Bell (video producer) and François Kevorkian (mixer) to Pino Pischetola (engineer), Billie Ray Martin (Electribe 101 singer) and Angela Shelton (dancer in the 'Halo' video), we've scoured the world, from Denmark to New Zealand via the US and Italy, to get unique and exclusive accounts of this amazing period in the band's history.

We thank them all.

Depeche Mode are, many argue, a very different phenomenon when you remove the legions of passionate fans from the equation. These people, fans from every walk of life, also have fascinating stories to tell about the 1989-1990 period in their lives, when 'Violator' consumed them.

Again, our huge gratitude for their enthusiasm for the project and for spending so much time thinking back to over 30 years ago for their amazing, often very personal contributions.

Our thanks must also go to Andy McMinn, Michael Rose, Linda Meijer and Markus Raebiger from the Depeche Mode Classic Photos And Videos group on Facebook. Their tireless work to document and archive every activity, image and clip associated with the band over a four-decade history is an extraordinary achievement and has been a wonderful resource for us. The same goes for those behind the wonderful Depeche Mode Live Wiki – another tremendous collection of information for fans.

We would also like to thank our editor Mat Smith, A. J. Barrett, who kindly agreed that we could use his iconic photograph (originally shot for the 'NME') as our front cover, and the team at Grosvenor House Publishing in the UK.

Finally, we are enormously grateful for all the ideas, tips, encouragement and cajoling from countless fans from across the world.

Also, to Depeche Mode, past and present, for providing some of the most enjoyable moments of our lives at their gigs and creating the music on 'Violator' (and at many other times during their career) that inspired us to write this book.

We sent the manuscript for 'Halo' to our editor the day before Andy Fletcher passed away on May 26, 2022, at the age of 60, so it seemed fitting – not least as 'World In My Eyes' from 'Violator' was frequently cited as his favourite Depeche Mode song – that we dedicate this book to him. RIP, Fletch.

David

Firstly, thank you to my wife Pam for all her love and support and for encouraging me to start the Almost Predictable Almost blog. Thanks, too, to Mum and Dad, Carolyn and Paul, Zoe and Thomas, Dave and the Almost Predictable Almost road crew of Stuart, John, John C, Jamie, Paul, Andrew and Colin. You have all put up with an awful lot! Also, thanks very much to everyone who has read the blog and shared its posts over the years. Finally, thank you to Kevin for inviting me to join him in writing this book. It has been a real privilege and an utter joy. The amount of work he has done on this book will ensure that even the most pedantic of Depeche Mode fans (people like me in other words) will treasure it.

Kevin

Thank you to all those who have picked me up far too often when times have been tough since starting this book. In particular, the long-suffering May clan of Claire, Ella and Sam, my folks back in Kent, Rob, Mark and the Hillmore Groove Gang, Duzzers, numerous colleagues and many more who I am now regrettably forgetting to mention – please forgive me. And, lastly and most importantly, my co-author and friend, David. His passion for Depeche Mode has been infectious and vital to the creation of this book.

Prologue

"I looked at Daniel... Both of us went 'this is a really, really, really good album'. We just had this feeling that we'd made something special."

***

Dave Gahan sits on the edge of a chair, head in his hands, shoulders wrapped in a white towel.

A member of the Depeche Mode entourage has an arm around him, listening intently and sympathetically, offering some words of comfort.

It is difficult to understand the details of the conversation between the two, nor perhaps are we really meant to, but Gahan is clearly utterly exhausted and very emotional.

This brief scene comes at the end of D. A. Pennebaker's feature-length rockumentary '101', a film made to commemorate Depeche's 'Music For The Masses' tour which ended in June 1988.

Pennebaker's crew had followed the antics of a group of fans as they made their way across the USA by bus, whilst simultaneously going behind the scenes with the band and the army of support people needed to keep the Depeche live act on the road.

It's a great movie and one which Pennebaker and partner Chris Hegedus later said was their most enjoyable film to make. In context, Pennebaker had previously made critically acclaimed films about Bob Dylan and had captured Jimi Hendrix at Woodstock.

For devoted fans and many others, '101' is a fascinating look at what it meant for the band as they toured relentlessly on the back of the success of their 1987 album, 'Music For The Masses'.

It was a long and gruelling tour for Depeche, but one that reaffirmed their status increasingly in the US as a brilliant live act with an arsenal of great songs.

The film brilliantly captures the emotions of the fans, as well as the band and its crew, covering everything from the elation after a gig to frustration over logistics.

It also portrays Depeche in an extremely human way – primarily in that, it has little of the gloss associated with traditional films of bands on the road.

Still, until '101', it was rather hard to truly understand what it was like to be involved in the Depeche machine, either as a band member or as part of its entourage.

Back to Dave...

His rather forlorn state came at the end of concert number 101, which inspired the band's Alan Wilder to suggest this as the title of the film and live album. It was a barn-storming celebration of a gig at the Pasadena Rose Bowl in LA, scheduled especially to mark the end of the tour.

The emotional release and physical exhaustion are obvious.

A tour of that size, across three continents, with hundreds of interviews, broadcast media appearances and after-show parties – as fun as the latter might sound – would obviously take their toll on even the hardiest musical road warriors, as Depeche had been throughout their career to that point.

A picture taken by Anton Corbijn on the sleeve for '101' shows Dave and the rest of the band, Andy 'Fletch' Fletcher, Wilder and Martin Gore, standing alongside Pennebaker; they all look completely shattered, yet also content and proud.

The four young men from England and the acclaimed filmmaker, are triumphant.

'101' was an appropriate finale to an important period for Depeche, encapsulated in those scenes from that final gig in LA.

In an interview in 2006, Gahan says, when referring to the Rose Bowl gig:

"It was pretty amazing. And there hasn't really been another concert like it... for us.

"Up until that point, this was our world. On some level that is what is so special about Depeche and everything that's gone on around it – we created our own sort of Utopia, and lived in it."

We also gain a hint of what triggered Gahan's tearful appearance at the end of '101'.He was visibly moved during the crowd's karaoke-like rendition of 'Everything Counts', leading him to add: "I had a strange feeling at that concert. I remember at the end of it, I really felt like it was all over.

"There was nowhere to go now with this caravan that we had been dragging around for the last ten years. What are we going to do now?"

Maybe Gahan is deliberately borrowing part of a line from the 1983 Depeche song 'And Then…', when he adds:

"It was almost like we had reached our destination," echoing the lines in the penultimate verse of the Gore-penned song from the album 'Construction Time Again':

When I reached my destination
I hadn't gone far

Clearly, Depeche had come a long way since releasing their debut single 'Dreaming Of Me' in February 1981.

But perhaps Dave, only 26 at this point, had a right to be worried about where Depeche would go next, even if such concerns were fuelled by the adrenalin of an emotionally charged gig.

Depeche were selling millions of records and performing to thousands of fans on a regular basis. However, the Rose Bowl gig could easily have been an appropriate cap on a successful career if the creativity dried up or if, conversely, Dave, Martin, Alan or Fletch had simply had enough.

Destination reached. Go out on a high.

Perhaps Dave couldn't envisage how he and Depeche could top something like the Rose Bowl concert, or the standard of songs such as 'Never Let Me Down Again' or 'Strangelove' from the 'Music For The Masses' album.

Dave's sometimes self-deprecating sense of humour has led him to say at least once that he's not particularly good at anything else. Exhaustion and fear of what might come next, however, are natural emotions for anyone at the end of a pivotal moment in their life.

"It changed after that – it had to, we had to take it to another level somehow."

***

It's the first weekend of August 1990, Dodger Stadium, Los Angeles, USA. Depeche have played two nights at the 50,000-capacity baseball venue, tickets for which sold out in a single day.

Earlier that week, on Wednesday night, the band played another gig – this time at the since-demolished Universal Amphitheatre.

A further 6,000 fans were treated, under the roof of what some claimed was one of the best venues for acoustics on the West Coast, to 'Strangelove' and 'Never Let Me Down Again', central songs of the setlist for the 'World Violation Tour'.

The latter song had become a live favourite for Depeche fans In part, this was because it was a great song, but, more often than not, it also ignited a celebratory mass waving of arms in the air by the crowd. When the spontaneous crowd response first happened on the 'Music For The Masses' tour, Gore remembered it being like a "field of wheat" swaying in the wind.

Yet, in a somewhat rare move for any band touring to support a recently released album, Depeche book-ended the main set at all three gigs with new songs.

The opener, 'World In My Eyes', was also the first track on the new long-player. Ending the set was a sing-a-long to rival 'Everything Counts': the album's first single, 'Personal Jesus'.

The final song from the encores on each night was a cover of a rock 'n' roll classic made famous by Nat King Cole and Chuck Berry, 'Route 66', which they had recorded for the B-side of the 'Behind The Wheel' single in 1987. Its inclusion spoke volumes about Depeche's new destination.

Here was essentially a synth band from Great Britain cranking out a loud, guitar-driven road tune to the masses.

They didn't need to perform former live favourites such as 'Just Can't Get Enough' and 'People Are People'.

Depeche had reached the new level that Dave had agonised over just three years before, such as the quality of the songs featured on the new album and the reaction to it from both fans and many critics.

Depeche, on stage in the heat of a South Californian summer in 1990, were a *tour de force*.

Then again, by this stage, no one seemed particularly surprised – save for some parts of the often sneering British music press. With these shows, the British music press reluctantly and finally realised their former whipping boys from the early-1980s were, in the words of then EMI records president Bruce Kirkland, "a legitimate, bona fide, arena headlining act in America – end of story".

The signs that something big - bigger even than the remarkable scenes captured in '101' – was happening to Depeche were there just six months before.

Los Angeles, again. The city features prominently – almost as much as the band's birth town of Basildon – in the history of Depeche, not least with it being where Dave later went through widely publicised brushes with death in the mid-1990s during his struggle with drug addiction.

The band arrived at The Wherehouse in downtown LA, for an in-store signing session, something that Alan would later describe as "the chore", ahead of the release of their new album.

To the apparent shock of the band, their entourage of publicists and security, Wherehouse's managers and, last but not least, the Los Angeles Police Department, an estimated 20,000 fans had descended on the area.

The disturbance which ensued as fans tried to get into the store was enough to thrust Depeche onto the evening news shows across America. Though it was downplayed by Alan at a press release after, the incident was understandably described as a riot.

The event illustrated what was about to happen to Depeche in 1990.

Their new destination – hinted at with the release of just two tracks, the aforementioned 'Personal Jesus' and second single 'Enjoy The Silence', unveiled just a few weeks before – came via a collection of tracks at a new level of creativity and depth compared to anything they had produced before. That new edge was, coupled with a clear and deliberately defined image and self-confidence.

Over three decades on and fans still, and always will debate their favourite segment in the now lengthy chronological record of the band and its music.

What few can argue against is that Depeche Mode, circa 1990, were at a fundamental – and easily the most important – point in their history. It was where, as Fletch says, they "hit the highs of sounds and songs".

Destination: 'Violator'.

Chapter 1

102

"I think that's one of the things that I've admired about them and I love about artists, in general, is when they try new stuff."

***

'101' was released in March 1989, in two formats: the film directed by D. A. Pennebaker and a double CD/vinyl LP/ cassette, which included the full set from the Pasadena Rose Bowl.

Depeche Mode fans had been wooed the month before its appearance with a live version of 'Everything Counts', taken from the album and released as a single.

By this stage in the band's career, each single would usually be released on a dizzying array of formats filled with remixes and B-sides.

The new version of 'Everything Counts' was no exception, with live versions of other songs from '101' thrown in, such as 'Nothing', and 'Sacred', both originally from the 'Music For The Masses' album.

There was also a remix of 'Everything Counts' from a 21-year-old Londoner by the name of Tim Simenon (Bomb The Bass) who later went on to produce Depeche's 'Ultra' album in 1997.

Still, despite the multiple formats, the single's highest chart position came in Germany, where it reached number 12.

The album '101',' on its release, hit positions 3, 4 and 5 respectively in the German, French and UK album charts, yet managed only a disappointing and remarkably low number 45 in the USA.

Perhaps Dave Gahan's concerns about Depeche's ability to evolve and, presumably, stay relevant in the eyes of their fans were already being played out, at least in the US where just nine months beforehand they had the world (well, approximately 66,000 fans in the Pasadena Rose Bowl) at their feet.

It was probably not the reason for the poor chart position for '101' in the US, but in that short, three-quarters of a year since the end of the 'Music For The Masses' tour in Los Angeles, music had started to change.

A look at fellow residents of '101' in the album charts in March 1989 would only give the merest of hints as to the shift starting to take place.

Yet in some respects, it was also a familiar story in the upper echelons of the pop world as the 1980s drew to a close.

Madonna's album 'Like A Prayer' was also released that month, hitting the number one spot in numerous countries.

Depeche rarely found themselves under the kind of scrutiny which Madonna seemed to attract (and court), but the singer -- with her new-found single status following her divorce from Sean Penn earlier in the year – was hardly off the front pages of newspapers and gossip magazines throughout the 1980s.

Yet, strangely, there was a connection between Madonna and how Depeche's 1989 could pan out.

The video for the single 'Like A Prayer' had triggered a bucket load of controversy due to its use of Catholic iconography and a dream sequence showing rather un-Catholic-like things taking place between Madonna and a saint.(Interestingly, the Anton Corbijn-directed video for Depeche's 'Walking In My Shoes' in 1993 does a pretty good job of hinting at playful behaviour between a nun and a priest, too.)

The Vatican wasn't particularly impressed with Madonna, and neither was Pepsi, who cancelled a lucrative branding tie-in with the singer.

It doesn't matter if Depeche took note or not (or, indeed, even cared) about Madonna's uncanny ability to bristle with the Roman Catholic Church and other Christian groups, whilst at the same time doing the marketing for her new single no harm at all.

Just eight months after the release of 'Like A Prayer', Depeche would find themselves in a similar situation when the first single from the as-yet-untitled new album appeared.

The band had previously found themselves in a spot of bother with the church over their songs 'Blasphemous Rumours' and 'Master and Servant'. Religion, suggestive behaviour and tongue-in-cheek videos were all lightning rods in the often prim worlds in which bands such as Depeche operate.

***

Thankfully, for every Madonna or Debbie Gibson, Jason Donovan or Simply Red which littered the charts in early 1989, there were also some stalwarts of the alternative music scene.

British electronic quartet New Order released the superb 'Technique' in February. The album buried most of the doubts some critics still held as to whether Barney Sumner – a name which will reappear later in the 'Violator' story and New Order could scale the creative heights of the Ian Curtis-fronted predecessor, Joy Division.

In May, fellow indie favourites The Cure also unleashed their best work to date, and still many fans' favourite album, 'Disintegration'.

Those lamenting the loss of The Smiths in 1987 were supposedly eagerly awaiting the next offering from a band who some argued was Morrissey and Johnny Marr's natural successor, at least musically, the House of Love.

Throw in Icelandic oddities The Sugarcubes and the dreamy, effects pedal-heavy combo, The Cocteau Twins, both of which were on the verge of releasing highly anticipated albums, and most critics could have been forgiven for their usual hyperbole if they said it was a landmark period for the more high profile end of independent music.

Over in the US, home traditionally in the 1980s to a depressing array of perm-heavy soft rockers, East Coast bands such as The Pixies and The Throwing Muses were grabbing plenty of attention. The Pixies released 'Doolittle' in April 1989, their follow-up to the debut album 'Surfer Rosa'.

Jane's Addiction were, despite dalliances with the usual rock 'n' roll excesses, expecting to release a new album that year, while The Rollins Band were noisily filling the gap left behind following the demise of Husker Dü a few years before.

Back across the Atlantic Ocean to continental Europe, the alternative scene was far more fragmented but had several vibrant and important players.

Depeche label-mates at Mute, Einstürzende Neubauten from Germany, and Belgian electronic outfit Front 242 had both achieved modest recognition outside of their home countries, in small part due to how often some critics mentioned them in the same breath when describing some of the musically edgier offerings from Depeche.These were the 'industrial' or 'EDM' outfits – labels some had already used with Depeche.

Yet many European bands of that ilk which were trying to get wider airplay were often compared unfairly with the pioneers of European electronic music, the almost 20-year-old Kraftwerk.

***

Perhaps the most significant, a wider musical trend to come to the fore by 1989, both in terms of its uniqueness and creativity, was the burgeoning dance music scene.

Correctly, many purists suggest the emergence of the dance scene in the late-1980s was, musically, just a logical extension of some of the disco tracks from the late-1970s.

Donna Summer's high-energy 1977 hit 'I Feel Love' could easily be considered a forerunner of house music given its standard 4/4 beat, big vocals and the use of synthesised sounds for the percussion.

In the early 1980s some of Chicago's club DJs, most notably Frankie Knuckles and Ron Hardy, started mixing disco and hip-hop tracks together on turntables, often overlaying them with their own beats, created on drum machines.

The music evolved to the extent that some of the tracks were given a professional touch by way of production and mixing, then pressed onto vinyl and distributed to other clubs in US cities such as New York and Detroit.

Some of the records found their way to clubbing hotspots in European cities such as Berlin and London. House music, as it was now known, was spreading.

The next significant leap in its evolution came in the mid-1980s when Marshall Jefferson scored a hit in the US and elsewhere with his track 'Move Your Body', a milestone which inspired fellow DJ Kevin Saunderson in Detroit to also create chart-friendly house tunes under the name Inner City a few years later.

Interestingly but perhaps not surprisingly, Inner City singles 'Big Fun' and 'Good Life' seemed to bypass the mainstream US entirely but were extremely popular in the UK.

Saunderson now says one of the records which often found its way onto the turntables of the Michigan clubs was the 12-inch version of Depeche's 1983 single 'Get The Balance Right'.

He and other DJs, such as Derrick May, a pioneer of house music, would loop particular segments of the song together or mix with other tracks.

It is perhaps difficult to put 'Get The Balance Right' on the pedestal that Saunderson has since given it as"the world's first techno record", though May acknowledges that the track became a huge US club hit.

Interestingly, fans of the record in the US had no real perception of the people – or band, in Depeche's case – that had created it, said May.

Depeche's 'image' on the US club scene was simply that of a name on a white label 12-inch record that would find its way to DJs via Sire Records.

It's rather ironic that a song which the band later didn't appear to particularly like, despite it being Alan Wilder's first as an official band member after a year or so as a gigging musician and one that wasn't featured on the 'Construction Time Again' album in the same year, is now cited as such an early influence on house music.

Still, Depeche's role as a player in the early world of dance music – a position, as we will see, that would mushroom after the 'Violator' period – had emerged.

It was a connection which Depeche appeared to be rather bemused by, although they – still slaves to the publicity machine which surrounded them – agreed to take part in what became an infamous meeting in the history of Depeche.

During a visit to the US in December 1988, to view some footage from the forthcoming '101' movie in New York, a meeting was arranged by 'The Face' magazine between Depeche and May.

May met with the band and, alongside journalist John McCready, gave them a tour of the famous Detroit underground club, The Music Institute. He also invited them to his apartment in the city, where he supposedly played them some tracks he was working on.

On the one hand, 'The Face' magazine had the quirky story of the British electronic act visiting "the best club on the planet", in the words of McCready, who had focused on the union between two entities placed at different parts of the musical and cultural spectrum.

In one part the article highlighted how the young lads from Britain, who were well known to partake in some extremely boozy nights out, appeared bemused by the alcohol-free club and the attention they received from some of its patrons.

In fact, Alan Wilder was particularly unimpressed by the entire experience, especially May.

He famously said later of his techno host in Detroit, "Derrick May was horrible – I hated him. He was the most arrogant fucker I've ever met. He took us into his backroom where he had a studio and played us this track, and it was fucking horrible."

It was a feature typical of 'The Face' – a wordy look at a clash of cultures, and an attempt to scrutinise the people behind their well-known, public faces.

McCready, a Brit, succeeded in the first part, but somewhat struggled to loosen the guard which surrounded Depeche after years of growing scepticism and disappointment with the media, especially those from home.

The reality of that period at the end of 1988 and early-1989 was rather different from that portrayed in the piece, namely that of a band riding the coattails of the hugely successful 'Music For The Masses Tour' in the US and the world seemingly at their feet.

Gahan's marriage to teenage sweetheart Joanne was unravelling and Fletch was going through his own battle with depression.

None of this was apparent in 'The Face', and there was no reason why it should have been.

Still, McCready's interview and article are an intriguing, and undoubtedly the most high profile, examination of where Depeche found themselves in the post-'Music For The Masses' period.

"Modus Operandum: Depeche Mode in Detroit", as the headline writers at 'The Face' put it when the article emerged in February 1989, was seized on by those eager to find out what the band was up to.

Somewhat vaguely, McCready wrote, "Alan Wilder tells me that the new material they are working on builds on the slower tempos of the 'Music For The Masses' LP."

In the same paragraph, reflecting on the hullabaloo created by the Detroit visit, Martin Gore was quoted as confessing, "We can't create dance music, and I don't think we've ever really tried. We honestly wouldn't know where to start."

Fans could have been forgiven at the time for thinking that Depeche were going to push further into exploring some of the darker, slower corners of their creative output from previous albums.

Perhaps the band would revisit the period that many critics, and Depeche's commercially minded people behind the scenes, believed to be Depeche's least accessible body of work, 1986's 'Black Celebration'.

'Music For The Masses' had been a triumph, especially in terms of "breaking America", but 'Black Celebration' had become a fans' favourite. One reason was that it had shown a new and distinct depth – with accompanying dark shadow – to Depeche in terms of songwriting and the diversity of the arrangements of the music.

The quartet of 'Fly On The Windscreen', 'Black Celebration', 'Stripped' and 'A Question Of Time' were arguably the best songs the band had ever recorded. Some would contend that these songs were leagues ahead of even the best tracks from the album's predecessor, 'Some Great Reward' from 1984.

Alternatively, maybe they would try replicating the formula and style of production which had inspired the strongest elements from 'Music From The Masses', such as 'Strangelove' and 'Never Let Me Down Again'.

The latter track in particular, despite not performing overly well in terms of chart position in many countries when it was released as the second single from the album, had become a favourite during the subsequent tour.

The truth was that very few outside of the traditionally closed ranks around the Depeche camp had much of an idea at all.

Any hints as to what might emerge by way of new material were hard to decipher from public comments. In part, this was because the band had to put aside what might be happening behind the scenes and embark on a merry-go-round of publicity to support the release of the '101' movie and accompanying album.

Sean Salo (USA), fan, admin on Home website and forum

As I write this in 2020, we are living amidst the coronavirus pandemic where self-isolation is the reality for much of the world.

We are Depeche Mode fans – we've been training for doom, gloom, and isolation our whole adolescent and adult lives! This crisis also makes me thankful for eras like these, upon which we can look back fondly and to which look forward after we have overcome what is hopefully a blip on our collective radars.

It's June 1990. The price to cross the George Washington Bridge from New Jersey into New York City was $3 and the toll booths caused miles of traffic during normal rush hours.

Even at midnight, crawling in 45 minutes of traffic to pay the bridge toll was not unexpected. But on that warm night in 1990, you could hear Depeche Mode pumping from the radio or tape decks all over the New Jersey Turnpike.

From a few lanes of traffic over from us, came a yell: "Sean! Yo, Sean! I knew I'd see someone else I knew here."

It was a frat kid from my university; Chad?... Brad? Before 1990, Depeche Mode had largely been a cult sensation in the United States. But that summer, you couldn't throw a rock into a frat house or at a line of cheerleaders without hitting someone who owned a copy of 'Violator'.

With nearly 80,000 other concert-goers all making their exodus from Depeche Mode's 'World Violation Tour' show at the old Giants Stadium back toward New York City, it was indeed a near certainty.

We arrived at the stadium later than I'd hoped. Admittedly, I underestimated the time it would take to get there. That didn't stop me from blaming everyone else in my crew who I had agreed to drive there.

We parked what felt like miles away, and as we made our way toward the entry gate, I could hear the opening percussion of Nitzer Ebb's 'Fun To Be Had' echoing through the parking lot.

I panicked and started to run, not wanting to miss a second more than I needed to, and my girlfriend at the time refused to join my trot, choosing to walk instead. (I'm not saying this was the reason we broke up, but it weighed heavily...)

I finally arrived at my seat on the floor of the stadium for the Ebb's third song of the set, 'Join In The Chant', just in time to see half of the crowd who'd been sitting or milling about feign fandom and jump to their feet for the song they knew from any of the dozens of dance clubs catering to synthpop, post-punk, and industrial music at the turn of the decade.

It was still bright as day when The Jesus and Mary Chain sauntered on stage with their set of fuzzy, feedback-laden noise. One might think this might be why they were gazing at their shoes throughout their set, but they were just staying true to form.

For the first half of 1990, they'd been playing largely in clubs and medium-sized venues, so the bright sun and open-air stadium was an atypical setting for them. While JAMC certainly had the catalogue and the name recognition, there was a noticeable drop in stage and crowd energy, even as the stadium continued to fill.

Many of us take for granted the experience of seeing Depeche in a stadium setting now, but in 1990, in North America,

Depeche Mode had yet to host audiences that large, east of the Los Angeles Basin.

Giants Stadium, home to American football's New York Giants and New York Jets, hadn't hosted many concerts up to that point, save for some stadium rock giants like Aerosmith, U2 and the hometown Jersey boy, Bruce Springsteen.

As a sign of the changing musical tastes of American young people, the last concert held before DM's 'World Violation Tour' date at Giants Stadium was a bit of a stunner, as well, with Love & Rockets, The Pixies and Shelleyan Orphan providing support for DM's contemporary, The Cure, on the 1989 'Prayer Tour' for their masterpiece, 'Disintegration'.

Still, The Cure required a mini-festival lineup to fill the stadium. Depeche Mode was largely carrying this show on their own, as JAMC and Nitzer Ebb only attracted a very niche lineup.

Proving they warranted the booking, 42,000 tickets sold on just the first day of sale, in an era where fans still had to queue up - many overnight - for hard tickets to be sold and printed at box offices and ticket selling locations.

The near-endless chatter and advertising created the feel of a not-to-be-missed event. Radio station 92.7 WDRE (aka WLIR) was an exclusive media promoter of the gig, and they broadcasted live from the venue throughout the afternoon leading up to the show, interviewing all three bands and highlighting their music throughout the day.

WDRE on-air presenter, Malibu Sue, later told me her quick thinking saved half of the duo.

"Nitzer Ebb opened the show - personally chosen by Depeche. I ended up saving one of the guy's necks – can't remember if it was Bon or Doug now – as he decided to crawl out the open window of the press box we were watching Depeche from and almost fell to his death! I grabbed him and pulled him back into the window!"

Sue's personal connection to the Giants Stadium show runs even deeper: "One of the fondest memories of my career was when the band only allowed me to go on-stage to intro them at Giants Stadium.

"The reception I got from our beloved listeners brought tears to my eyes. Looking out over a crowd of about 80,000 was daunting, to say the least, and I was very grateful to the band for the opportunity! I was so touched and overwhelmed, that I barely choked out 'I love you' to the crowd. It was exhilarating."

The Giants Stadium show was certainly momentous for Depeche Mode and their fans. It also proved monumental in shaping other bands' histories. Anton Corbijn introduced 'Violator' producer Flood to Bono and Adam Clayton in the press box, which led to Flood's production of U2's iconic 'Achtung Baby' album.

Flood recalled a pivotal meeting at the show for U2.com: "Depeche Mode were playing Giants Stadium (after we'd recorded 'Violator' together) and I was sitting on my high throne in the press box, getting absolutely mullered, thinking, 'How good does this get?', when Anton Corbijn says: 'Flood, I have a couple of people to see you.' These two scruff-bags with hoodies and a beard walk through the door, and it's Bono and Adam, in disguise. So we were all there, having a few jars, and they said, 'We want to blow up the old U2 and go to Berlin to make a new record. Are you interested?'

"The band [U2] couldn't go back to where they were - that was the overriding philosophy. They were saying to me, 'Be as free as you want to be. Try everything!' I'd been working with Depeche and Nine Inch Nails, so they were looking for some of that 'industrial' input."

Having already seen Depeche Mode on the 'Black Celebration' and 'Music for the Masses' tours, I wasn't prepared for the spectacle of seeing them in a stadium setting.

The 50-foot high stage rigging dangled similarly gargantuan roses flanking stage left and right. The sun was still setting in the early summer sky as the opening house music thumps of 'Kaleid' began pulsating, sending the crowd into a frenzy.

It was the perfect intro to prep the crowd for the bass-heavy 'World In My Eyes' show opener. This and the five tunes that followed ('Halo', 'Shake The Disease', 'Master And Servant' and 'Never Let Me Down Again') could've stood on their own as a perfect intro to DM mixtape.

'Waiting For The Night' gave us our first chance to catch our collective breaths and take in the vocal duo of Dave Gahan and Martin Gore. The acoustic set of 'I Want You Now' and 'World Full Of Nothing' followed.

'Clean' bookended the acoustic set and provided the last chance for any butts-in-seats for the evening.

The setlist for this tour has been obsessed over, especially in the absence of an official live recording release. But the remainder of the set that evening was all-killer / no filler.

As my friends and I made our way back to my car, drenched in sweat from the second encore's one-two punch of 'Behind The Wheel' and 'Route 66', we were still in awe of what we'd just witnessed. Happily, I'd have another opportunity a couple of nights later to see Nitzer Ebb's full set with their only theatre show of the North American leg, at Radio City Music Hall.

Ironically, 'Violator' and the 'World Violation Tour' marked both the height and the end of the era for synth-pop in America as the Madchester genre became the flavour of the year on alternative radio, which had long been the home for all things Depeche.

Just over a year after the Giants Stadium show, grunge rock started to make the technical and songwriting brilliance of 'Violator' seem increasingly out-of-place on the radio format DM helped build.

The show at Giants Stadium, however, will always stand out as a pinnacle event in my decades of fandom.

Chapter 2

Getting Out Of Your Own Way

"This scruffy, bespectacled, rather unlikely-looking bloke rolled up, raided the fridge a couple of times, slouched down on the sofa, pontificated for a bit and, thus, a new production team was born."

***

'Music For The Masses' was the first album where Depeche Mode had stepped away from the relative comfort zone of a production team which, until then, had always featured Mute boss Daniel Miller as both their family-like guiding hand and producer in the studio.

Miller had produced the band's first two albums, 'Speak And Spell' and 'A Broken Frame', with the band, in part because he was the only person within the Depeche camp that had any experience in a recording studio.

They later hired the energetic Gareth Jones to engineer 'Construction Time Again' in London – a decision which in part inspired a period of intense experimentation with the then-somewhat fledgling use of sound sampling to augment the synthesiser-led melodies in Martin Gore's demos.

Jones was later given a full production credit alongside Miller for 1984's 'Some Great Reward' and 'Black Celebration' in 1986.

The union of the band, Miller and Jones, in many respects, solidified the Depeche 'sound' during that mid-1980s period, with the diverse array of bizarre samples by then forming not only the rhythm elements of songs but also large swathes of melody and atmosphere.

Jones's addition to the studio line-up in 1983 also coincided with the band's decision to start working in overseas studios.

All three of the Berlin Trilogy long-players, as they're sometimes called, were in part recorded or mixed at the famous Hansa Studios in Berlin, with Gore infamously putting the vocal down for 'Some Great Reward's ballad 'Somebody' wearing nothing but his nail varnish in one of its vast, echoing rooms.

This strategy of heading overseas not only got the band out of the UK, but it set a precedent for how most of the band's albums would be recorded in the future. In part, this was a deliberate move to expose them all – band and production team – to other cultures and musical styles away from London, as well as simply giving them different surroundings to enjoy themselves in and get some breathing space from the inevitable pressure that would build with each new Depeche release.

Sonically, Depeche were still almost exclusively an electronic band, both in terms of their output and the perception of them by their fans and the industry.

Though it was not necessarily heralded at the time, eventually this period would be considered pioneering by many for the sampling techniques Depeche were using to form the creative backbone of their songs.

On all of these albums, driven primarily by Miller, Jones and Alan Wilder – the member of the band who by his own admission most enjoyed being in the studio and was by then playing a very active role in the mechanics of putting their songs together – Depeche would spend large amounts of time in the studio (or outside) sampling themselves hitting or rolling whatever they could get their hands on, to then place into songs.

It worked.Depeche's sound became increasingly industrial yet still retained the catchy melodies of the early days to ensure the songs were accessible but included a depth that mirrored the growing confidence Gore had found to explore the darker and more intense ideas he had that were contained within his songwriting.

The success of 'Construction Time Again', 'Some Great Reward' and 'Black Celebration' brought gradual changes in the Depeche camp.

Throughout the five albums in which he helmed the production duties for Depeche in the studio, Miller was still somehow managing to simultaneously run Mute Records and also produce some of the other artists on the label.

But by 1986, artists such as Frank Tovey, Nick Cave & The Bad Seeds, Mark Stewart and Crime and The City Solution were turning Mute into a modestly successful independent record label.

This period also marked the emergence of the wonderfully poppy Erasure, another two-piece created by ex-Depeche founder Vince Clarke who quit in 1981 and formed Yazoo with Essex pal Alison Moyet. Though that duo's existence was fleeting, they were even more successful than the band Clarke had left.

The reluctant pop star still had a knack for finding himself back in the limelight due to his incredible ability to create perfect, chart-bound songs for his creative partners.

But even with Depeche now turning out an album of fresh material, by then, every 18-24 months, rather than the one-year cycle of their early days, by late-1986 Mute couldn't spare Miller to spend three days in the studio with Depeche, let alone the three months that it had taken to record and mix 'Black Celebration'.

The 'Black Celebration' sessions, recorded at Berlin's Hansa and London's Westside and Genetic Studios, were especially tense and drawn out.

Miller and Jones had put forward the idea that the band and production team would "live the album", a process by which everyone would dutifully come to the studio every single day until the project was complete.

An extremely claustrophobic environment was inevitable given the conscious decision to create an intense and different type of working environment, giving rise to what most fans at the time agreed - 'Black Celebration' was clearly Depeche's darkest piece of work to date.

Putting aside the critical acclaim from fans and even some critics, 'Black Celebration' was a huge turning point in many respects.

The production team and band had gone through the process of making three extremely important albums together, but the experience of doing so was starting to take its toll – not least because the creation of *Black Celebration* had been a lengthy one and at times the self-imposed environment had started to cause tensions in the camp.

Miller was, by now, firmly established as the band's father figure, with Jones the somewhat cheeky yet encouraging uncle. Despite creating and achieving so much together in terms of successful records, Depeche wanted – and needed – to move on creatively.

There was also a certain dissatisfaction with the final quality of the production of 'Black Celebration', with Wilder claiming the mixes sounded "odd - too much reverb, not enough bottom end, etc".

Those reasons, coupled with Miller's "other job" running Mute Records, coincided with the selection of Dave Bascombe as a producer for the next record.

Mute and the band had "really liked the sound he got with Tears For Fears and other things he'd done", Miller later told 'Electronic Beats'.

Bascombe was seen as a highly rated, up-and-coming engineer having worked on Tears For Fears' Songs From The Big Chair' album in 1985. It was his work on that album that had caught Depeche's ear, as well as his work with Echo And The Bunnymen.

Miller said: "We picked the studio – we wanted to get away from Berlin, but we didn't want to do London, so we found a really nice studio in Paris.

"I went there for the first couple of days to make sure everybody was comfortable and it was all working okay; I remember the feeling of an incredible weight off my shoulders knowing I wasn't going to be in the studio with them for the next six months!

"I remember walking out of the studio, it was a sunny day, I thought, 'They're going to make a record, I'm not going to be there, and it's going to be a much better record for it and I'm going to feel much better for it, as well.'

"Dave Bascombe was very good at translating the ideas into reality, so they made a good team."

Given the five months that it took to make and size of the sound that emerged on 'Music For The Masses' – especially on songs such as 'Never Let Me Down Again' – the album's production team was relatively small in size compared to its predecessor.

Many of the tracks on 'Music For The Masses' are expansive and confident in style, perhaps reflecting Bascombe's input, and leading some to remark how close the overall feel of the record was to the Tears For Fears classic of a few years before.

Still, Wilder claimed that, of all the Depeche albums he was involved in, 'Music For The Masses' was probably the most self-produced record.

"With all due respect, Dave Bascombe's role was more as a good engineer rather than producer."

Gone was the somewhat youthful playfulness of the Berlin era albums, with noticeably fewer samples and an obvious depth to the musicality within the arrangements.

It was almost as if all the hard work of discovering they had a dark side to their music and Gore's songwriting was fulfilled on 'Black Celebration', and now it was time to start spreading their wings a little.

Yet it was pretty remarkable to many that the expansive new sound of 'Music For The Masses', regardless of whether it was fuelled by self-assurance, a new production unit or something else, was less than two years on from the loathed single 'It's Called A Heart', a release the band very quickly sought to distance themselves from.

As the 'Music For The Masses Tour' was rolling along to its glorious conclusion during the spring and early summer of 1988, thoughts in some quarters were already starting to turn to how the next phase might come together.

By this time there was no room for sentimentality with individuals that had helped Depeche achieve success with a particular album.

Depeche Mode, by then really beginning to realise their potential and understanding of how different people managed to push them a little bit further each time they recorded new material, knew they had to push again.

Miller said: "We wanted to keep moving on from *Music For The Masses*, even though that had worked out very well. I think everybody had felt that the fresh blood at that time had really pushed things along and we wanted to do that again. And Flood seemed like an obvious choice."

***

How does one describe the formation of what Gore later labelled the "great team" that was assembled to create Depeche Mode's much-anticipated follow-up to *Music For The Masses*?

Alan Wilder describes when Depeche Mode first officially met with the unkempt and forthright Flood in his typically low-key and somewhat dour way.

The reality is that the "scruffy, bespectacled" Flood had been gradually working himself into the consciousness of those who felt Depeche should take another significant step forward in the way their music was created.

London-born Mark Ellis was given the nickname 'Flood' pretty early on his career as an assistant in various studios, apparently for his ability to appear with cups of tea (or spilling them) for artists and producers as he worked his way up through what was then a well-trodden and defined hierarchical path for junior members of a facility.

He quickly raised his profile on the production scene and developed a reputation as a talented all-rounder at Battery Studios, liked for his technical prowess with the growing array of technology that was making its way into the modern studio such as samplers and computers. He also established confidence in being able to put forward his own melodic and rhythmic ideas that would then be incorporated into an artist's songs.

Mute Records recognised his talent early on, giving him a selection of engineering and production duties on various Nick Cave & The Bad Seeds albums in the mid-1980s, including 'From Here To Eternity' and 'Kicking Against

The Pricks', as well as a mix of Fad Gadget's 'Collapsing New People'.

The Depeche Mode connection officially started when he engineered 'Shake The Disease' for its 1985 single release, and a year later when he was behind the Highland Mix of 'Stripped'.

Higher profile credits for the camera-shy, 24-year-old Flood followed when he produced 'Wonderland', Erasure's debut album.

He had essentially become Mute's go-to guy for studio duties for many of the label's roster of bands, but he was also starting to catch the eye of forces outside of the electronic world.

Flood's burgeoning reputation during this period at the hugely respected Trident Studios in London, and when he later left to go freelance, saw him end up working with a band metaphorically miles away from Mute's stable of synth-based acts.

Ros Earls, the owner of producer management agency 140db, said in an interview: "There were two groups of people who really noticed it. One was Daniel Miller at Mute, and the other was U2. Those two groups of people could see what he had. That he had something magical, and it wasn't about Trident.

"I don't know how U2 found out about him. The rumour mill, I expect. It wasn't about the room (Trident). It was about him."

In 1987, the same year as producing Erasure's second album 'The Circus', Flood was asked to join the studio team as an engineer for U2's 'The Joshua Tree'.

Despite achieving enormous success with their previous albums, 'The Joshua Tree' took the Dublin quartet to superstardom around the world with its blend of Brian Eno and Daniel Lanois atmospheres, guitars and deliberate nods toward traditional American and Irish music.

Such was its impact that 'The Joshua Tree' helped cement lead singer Bono's status as a rock icon of the era and, sales-wise, was a chart-topper around the world.

'The Joshua Tree' may have been Eno and Lanois' finest moment with U2, but it also helped ensure Flood's name would be on the list of leading studio people in demand as the 1980s came to a close.

Still, 'The Circus' was seen by many as the record where Flood's influence as more than just as a studio whizz could be felt.

Earls said: "He [Flood] really dislikes that you can hear him on the record, and he would deny it until the cows come home, but I think we all know where he's been.

"In Flood's mind, he takes it very seriously that a producer doesn't flaunt his ego above the ego of the band. He's a collaborative person. Yes, U2 was different, it was more collaborative. When he worked with Eno, he was more collaborative.

"He is collaborative but (as his career evolved) he started to spread his wings, and grow himself. Those (two albums) were the first signs of what he was capable of."

Production duties started pouring in over the next few years, with him steering albums for Nitzer Ebb ('Belief'), Pop Will

Eat Itself ('This Is The Day... This Is The Hour... This Is This!') and Renegade Soundwave ('Soundclash'), as well as some tracks on the debut album from Nine Inch Nails, 'Pretty Hate Machine'.

Flood's work with Nine Inch Nails and Pop Will Eat Itself were perhaps the biggest hints at things to come elsewhere in his catalogue of production credits, given their fusion of guitars with an electronic sound.

Nevertheless, Flood has over the years steadfastly refused to entertain the idea that he has a 'sound' of his own or a trademark style that listeners can easily identify as belonging to him.

Flood may not have some kind of musical signature, but there are plenty of clues to his approach in the studio and the way he manages the recording process.

One of his most vocal fans over the years is Billy Corgan, frontman of The Smashing Pumpkins, the US guitar band that had three albums produced by Flood and long-time collaborator Alan Moulder.

Corgan said in an interview with 'Guitar Center': "Flood is very masterful with the sonics, but where he really shines is he's a great idea person. And I don't mean like he tells you, 'Oh, put this chorus here.'

"It's more like he can see an ambience of the song that you don't necessarily see and he would really fight with us – not a negative fight, just he would really kind of push us to say there's another vibe here that you can get to."

Flood's ability to push artists in different, but not definitive, ways was becoming a hallmark of the bands that he was working with.

It wasn't a particular style around certain sounds or even the approaches that he would use in the studio, at least from a technology or instrumentation perspective, but a technique - a way in which he gave a recording process a culture all of its own.

He was able to create an environment that allowed bands to breathe in a way that they may not have been used to, perhaps due to their management or record company having preconceived ideas of how their material should sound compared to previous releases; or, equally, because the songwriters were too afraid to take themselves out of a self-held comfort zone when it came to reproducing their raw material into something that, in the recorded form, could damage what they considered to be how they should sound.

By luck or design, or a mixture of the two when the benefit of hindsight is added into the analysis, Flood has found himself working with artists at critical moments in their careers.

It is, in fact, something that has continued throughout his production career, whether as an overarching producer or as an important gear in the overall studio machine as a record mixer or engineer.

The list is impressive: U2, The Smashing Pumpkins, The Jesus and Mary Chain, PJ Harvey, and even Welsh crooner Tom Jones.

Alan Wilder said of the reasons why Flood was brought on board: "I think we were reassured that Flood was able to do all things. He was able to be very hands-on; he could work a sampler; he could use an analogue synth.

"He could also come up with ideas – musical ideas, rhythm ideas; and [do] very specific, what we ended up calling screwdriver work."

"And at the same time, he could take a back seat overview and," adopting a deep tone, "be your Svengali-type: 'This is what you need to do boys'."

In short, according to Wilder, Flood was: "An all-around, good producer."

***

The other new and equally important addition to the studio team was François Kevorkian, a gentle 34-year-old from France who had relocated to the US in the mid-1970s.

After making a name for himself as a DJ on the New York club scene, especially in legendary venues such as Studio 54 and Paradise Garage, Kevorkian quickly boosted his credentials as a mixer and producer, most notably on Sharon Redd's 'Beat The Street' and 'Keep On' by D-Train.

Away from the disco world, Kevorkian had caught the eye of Daniel Miller who, alongside former Depeche Mode songwriter Clarke, then asked him to create a 12-inch remix of Yazoo's 'Situation' in 1982.

The song was originally set as the B-side to the group's second single in the UK, 'Don't Go', but Kevorkian's mix was released in its own right in the US alongside the 7-inch version.

The track became popular on alternative radio stations and topped the Billboard Hot Dance Club Play chart, as well as being included in a list of the best singles of the year in the New York newspaper, 'The Village Voice'.

Kevorkian's stock increased further when he was asked to mix Kraftwerk's labour of love, 'Electric Cafe', an album which took four years to complete in various stages and eventually achieved only modest commercial success.

Legend has it, at the very end of the production process and following several previously aborted attempts by the band to mix the album, Kraftwerk co-founder Ralf Hütter flew to New York with the master tapes so that he and Kevorkian could complete the record together at the city's Right Track studios.

'Electric Cafe' probably managed to do more for Kervorkian's career than it did for Kraftwerk's, having established him not only as someone who could be trusted by the famously insular German electronic outfit but coinciding with his growing reputation as a pioneer of house music.

Alan Wilder in particular was an admirer of Kraftwerk's output at the time. Along with Kevorkian's history with Yazoo and Daniel Miller, in some respects, it was only a matter of time before he would be approached to work with Depeche in some way.

In fact, such a partnership could have happened before the summer of 1988, when Kevorkian first sat down with the band and Flood. The year before, he was asked to produce a DJ mix intended for the US 12-inch release of 'Behind The Wheel' that would blend the single seamlessly together with its B-side, 'Route 66', but could not commit the time to its execution

The medley that Kevorkian was asked to turn his hand to was eventually pulled together by a producer / DJ by the name of Ivan Ivan and released in December 1987. Nevertheless, the appetite for Depeche to work with Kevorkian was established.

Undeterred by the scheduling conflicts that prevented collaboration in 1987, Depeche clearly wanted Kevorkian to be involved by the time discussions were underway to recruit people for the follow-up album to 'Music For The Masses'.

Reputations can be unkind and misinterpreted, even if they do have a degree of accuracy, as Depeche would later discover, but Kevorkian was a vital figure in the what was to emerge throughout the second half of 1988 as Depeche began to consider how they would approach their next collection of recordings.

***

It could have been very easy for Depeche Mode, as the 'Music For The Masses' period came to a sharp yet glorious halt in the June of 1988, to stick to the mantra of 'if it ain't broke, don't fix it'.

Indeed, rhetorically, why radically change the style of a band that was by this point able to produce commercially successful albums and go on the road for months at a time and play to arenas and huge stadiums, as the Pasadena Rose Bowl gig had proven?

Such deliberations have dogged bands throughout the history of music, but they come into focus in a more acute way when commercial success has been achieved and there is, in some minds at least, greater risk and therefore more to lose if the wrong turn is taken.

Depeche, in particular, were at the stage of being able to easily pay the bills on their side of the rather unique, supposed 'handshake' contract they had with Mute Records – a 50-50 split on costs upfront, with a likewise share of the rewards – and also finally make some decent money for themselves, as Gahan said at the time.

In fact, even at this stage in their career, there was still a club-like, informal feel around how the Depeche machine was pulled together and dragged around the world.

Names that had been associated with the band for many years were still around. Daniel Miller, of course, plus tour director and sound chief J. D. Fanger, booking agent Dan Silver, radio plugger Neil Ferris, production manager Andy Franks, PR man Chris Carr and Daryl Bamonte, a friend of the band from Basildon and their assistant in various guises since the beginning. Gahan's wife Joanne, who had given birth to the couple's son Jack in 1987 helped run the official Depeche Mode Fan Club from their home in the UK.

Yet despite the size of the team working for the band when they were on the road, and the complexity of the operation required to produce, distribute and promote a new release, Depeche still felt in many respects like a family business.

Other bands – especially those with such a close-knit culture within the inner circle, many of whom would inevitably be cautioning against deviating from what had become a well-trodden path to success and security – would've been averse to any sudden, or even slight, change.

But that wasn't Depeche's style – indeed, in some respects, it never had been.

They had always challenged themselves, sometimes out of necessity, often out of stubbornness.

When founding member Vince Clarke left the band at the end of 1981, sticking to the original formula of three-minute pop songs, which Gore was more than capable of writing, would have been easy, though perhaps not as long-lasting.

When other bands had decided the risk (and cost) of travelling east behind the old Iron Curtain, to cities such as Prague, wasn't one worth taking in the 1980s, Depeche did so because they knew they had fans there that were listening to their music.

Still, these were risks that still did not fundamentally change how they were perceived, by their fans, critics and probably even themselves – that of being an electronic band that could pump out largely synth-based music that was extremely well-produced but extremely structured and secure in its own creativity.

By 1988, many could be forgiven for wondering where Depeche Mode could go next as recording artists.

***

The choice of Flood to lead the production team for the next "project" was one – but an extremely significant – part of the band's two fingers to what many might have expected to be the follow-up to the 'Music For The Masses' album.

Dave Bascombe's involvement with the band had helped create two of Depeche's most accomplished songs so far in their eight-year history: 'Never Let Me Down Again' and 'Strangelove'.

But that was too easy – there was a feeling that post-'Music For The Masses', this was a unique time to really challenge themselves, or at least allow themselves to be challenged by a producer who knew which buttons to press, metaphorically and technically, to get the best out of people.

Miller and the band had sensed the opportunity was finally there because they knew Flood was desperate to work with the band, Kevorkian was finally available, and Gore had written a collection of songs that, to the closed ranks of the few who had heard the demos, were at a far higher level of maturity and originality than he'd shown so far.

As Miller explained of the thought process at the time: "This is the record we want to make now and let's make it. It was about getting followers to understand what the band were about and not repeating themselves.

"Let's take the fans with us – we've got good fans, they're smart, don't pander to them, let's experience something new together. An overall philosophy."

François Kevorkian (USA), studio mixer on 'Violator'

Depeche Mode had been trying to work with me for quite a long time, and for whatever reason, it wasn't easy.

I was always busy on one project or another which made it difficult.

For example, they had wanted me to do a remix of 'Behind The Wheel' and I had to actually pass it on to someone else.

I went to the studio to listen to them and I thought, "Wow, this is great. I would love to work on this."

They wanted to do some sort of medley of 'Behind The Wheel' and 'Route 66', put together as one track, and they asked me to do it.

I thought this would really be nice as I just love the recording. It was so well-produced and tight. But I just couldn't do it.

Basically, it all came together in the summer of 1988.

A beautiful English summer, that's what I can remember, really, as all of us got together at a pub – Martin, Dave, Alan, Fletch and Flood. I think it was near Martin's house.

It was really casual, very friendly, very mellow.

Back in those days, Alan was taking a reasonably strong role.

I was pretty much under the impression that the reason why they called me was that Alan was fixated on some of the things I had been doing with Kraftwerk.

I was just on the heels of having finished mixing their newest studio album, 'Electric Cafe', as well as a lot of the 12-inches.

Besides that, also, I had a track record with Mute Records because I had previously done the US remix of the Yazoo song, 'Situation'.

It turned into a really massive hit stateside. Daniel Miller and I had pretty much already dealt with each other a bit.

We certainly were keenly aware of who was who and what the other did, and so on.

The thing about Kraftwerk is that they raised the issue of privacy to previously hitherto unknown heights.

So I was obviously one of the very few outside collaborators who kept coming back and doing more stuff with them.

So I think that probably intrigued Depeche.

I got the impression that Martin is really always concerning himself with the bigger picture of the music – the songwriting, the overall vibe or the aura.

So I felt that, to Martin, my connections with Kraftwerk were almost just technical details. I think Flood was sort of a bit in-between.

But Alan Wilder was certainly the one who was clearly and strongly supporting the idea of having me become part of the team for the album mix.

It was very clearly spelt out that they were going to call me when the first single was ready.

They wanted me to do the single. If everything went well then we would just do the rest of the album as well.

I was obviously dying to work with them. I loved all the stuff they were making but it had just been very difficult to get our schedules together. So of course when we got together that afternoon and sort of talked about it, I had a lot of expectations that we were going to finally get something going on.

The band were on the heels of '101'. The movie put them over the top with the American audiences in a way that was remarkable because, for whatever reason, it presented Depeche Mode not just as some other electronic music act.

In a lot of people's eyes, Depeche Mode were now a big, stadium-touring rock band.

The band were going to do some recording and some production.

And then they were going to send me unfinished demos of the songs for me to start getting my head around what they were working on and send back some ideas.

***

I remember the week that I arrived in Milan was when the events happened in Tiananmen Square in China.

Flood had done his mixes of 'Personal Jesus', so it just needed more from me.

It was a pretty epic production. And a very unusual thing. They didn't have a drum set. It was the sound of people's footsteps doing the rhythm – a very different approach but a great one at that. We did all sorts of things.

Rather than just doing a single or an album mix, we also did 12-inch versions which took quite a while longer.

Because of that, we did some additional production recording which is always great when you have the band there at the same time. They can change things as they need to be changed and so on.

It was a pretty complex and involved situation, technically, with a lot of tracks, and these were back in the days when tape machines were involved.

Towards the end of that mix, I didn't even go back to the hotel. I just stayed in that studio until the thing was finished.

I would sleep on the couch and doze off a little bit, then keep working and take another nap.

Sometimes it would be difficult to have to constantly explain to someone else what to do. Often, it would be a lot easier for me to just do it!

But the engineers were obviously vital – listening in different environments, different speakers – perhaps at first being in the car, or playing the track on another sound system.

The engineer is obviously very important for that. It's crucial, actually. Because if I got too caught up in that part of it, chances are I probably wouldn't do very good at it.

***

I really didn't add a hell of a lot at all to the single version of 'Personal Jesus'.

Most of the additional production or extra work that we did was all for the remixes, for the 12-inch and the dub version.

It was really well-organised. It wasn't one of those multi-tracks where you had so many choices and so many things to sort through.

The song was already well-laid out, well-arranged. There really wasn't a hell of a lot that could be changed about it.

Flood really wasn't there very much because he was busy doing the production for the rest of the album, and so on.

Obviously, he passed by when he was there. He gave it a nod and he took a listen to what we were doing. Everybody seemed pretty much in sync with each other.

The band would come in and check in every so often, to see what progress was made or if there was something that needed to be looked at and explained.

Daniel Miller also came by a couple of times. And then they had the engineer from the studio [Pino Pischetolo] who was more or less acting as an all-around helper for the session.

Dennis Mitchell, an engineer, came with me from New York, too.

The context, the direction that 'Personal Jesus' took was implicitly the right direction because it presented them more as a rock band.

To me, that was the thing that really stood out. The fact that they have the slide guitar in there.

Even though it's not a guitar solo or a big guitar part, like a normal rock band – one of those normal guitar rock bands would have, say the Steve Miller Band or AC/DC, where it's clearly a huge guitar-fest.

It was more subtle in the case of Depeche Mode. Also, the drum sound that I usually associate with an electronic music act is very synthetic-like but because of the footsteps on 'Personal Jesus', plus the guitar, these really gave it more of a live feel.

It was a very important aspect of the way the single should come out.

I would also say the sound of the vocal was very important.

Flood was experimenting with different microphones. But on this particular song, they found that a cheap Shure SM57 mic sounded the best because it had more of this grungy feel to it.

It gave Dave's voice a vibe that, again, much more closely matched some of these big American rock records.

It wasn't said like that but I think, even though we weren't discussing it in those terms, for me the underlying theme was this because of the way the song was structured and the feeling of it.

It was kind of implied that it needed to have a bit more of a hybrid approach rather than a full electronic music kind of atmosphere about it.

We wanted more of a real pop and rock record – probably not what the average Depeche Mode fan would have expected them to come up with as their new single.

***

I already had my schedule pretty much set once they decided that we should go forward and do the rest of the album together.

They were obviously very happy with the way it turned out and they were just looking forward to doing more of the same.

That was taken before the single was released, whether it was a success or not.

For something to be such a success, it actually does take a while. It's not instant.

I don't think that when they decided to ask me to do the rest of the album they necessarily had a full assessment of the impact of 'Personal Jesus'.

There had to be a lot of planning. They had to book the studio, they had to make all these arrangements with their own schedules.

By the time I was brought back in, mostly everything was complete.

There were a few things to touch up which happened at the Church studio in London.

A couple of times, they asked me to take a couple of hours off as they needed to redo something really quick or something like that – things I didn't need to necessarily even be involved in.

The only time there was any pressure on me was when they wanted 'Enjoy The Silence' rather quickly because they knew it was going to be the second single.

They only had a certain window available and that's what it had to be. There was actually a little bit of a conflict with my schedule – I had to get back to New York.

Consequently, even though I had been working on it quite a bit, I ended up having to leave with the single not quite finished.

They decided to kind of redo it themselves in the end.

I did a mix but it was not quite as convincing as it should have been and they took a stab at it themselves with Daniel, so that's the version they ended up using.

I was obviously trying to be as open-minded and creatively available as possible with regards to allowing them to have it done however they felt.

It was their record, not mine. I never really had the feeling that it was my place to tell them, "Well, no. This needs to be done like this or like that."

Yet I don't ever recall at any single instance of any sort of friction of sort or anything of that sort.

***

The thing about working with Depeche Mode is that they're not just professional – they're really smooth, really fun and nice to work with, too.

And certainly not the kind of people that you feel like, "Oh, my God. I'm going to dread this and have to go back to the studio."

It was always really positive – and they were very sensible and reasonable. They just let me do whatever I wanted!

Often I would get a joke from Martin because he was not very interested in the minute details of what I was doing. He just wanted to make a great song and have the performance and the feeling of it come out the way he intended it to be.

That's really what Martin cared about more than anything.

I felt that this was a really important project. And whereas maybe in a normal set of circumstances, I probably would have not cared about certain details.

But it was a very important step in their career and so, in my own case, a lot of my contributions were going to be in bringing all the details and the atmosphere and everything together in a way that I wanted to give a sense of timelessness.

A lot of that becomes minute little adjustments and things that you might not hear the twentieth time you hear the record, but you'll hear it the hundredth time.

To that effect, I had hired the best people – the ones who I felt were the most qualified to do the work.

For example, I started the project with a Japanese engineer called Goh Hotoda, who was on the staff at my studio. He is a really brilliant person who also happens to exhibit the very same qualities – extremely meticulous and attention to detail to an incredible degree.

It certainly did take a fair amount of time and sometimes I was being very particular about specific things that I was trying to achieve.

Or, other times, for example, I was trying to get more direction from the band as to what they'd like me to do.

This was interesting because, at times, I felt that Martin purposely liked things to be vague – but not in a bad way.

I'm sure he's had this conversation with many people, but sometimes I would ask him, "Well, what is this lyric supposed to mean because it's rather ambiguous? It's sort of awkward for me not to know what I'm supposed to be mixing."

He would just say, "Well, that's because I wrote it like this by design!"

He was trying to write lyrics that sometimes were vague enough that people could use them as a fantasy that they would then illustrate themselves.

I thought that was incredibly clever - that you could write lyrics that would allow people to make their own versions.

They almost have an abstract quality about them. That's incredible.

I had never encountered anyone who was doing it consciously so much as he did. I was really awestruck by that.

An illustration of this would be the way the video for 'Enjoy The Silence' turned out. I would never in a million years have thought of those images for it – but someone else did.

But sometimes I would be trying to get a little bit of guidance from them and I would be humorously reminded that "well, it's whatever you want it to be!"

I didn't feel that I should try to illustrate the songs in any particular manner. So I was trying to come up with treatments that would still allow for what Martin wanted, rather than being overly specific.

A lot of times, when you're mixing albums, you really sweat about little details because they are going to be replicated thousands or millions of times and you have to make sure.

So I felt that what I did was certainly appropriate for the circumstance.

***

Flood and I never really spent a lot of time together because when we were mixing, he was busy with other things or was elsewhere. We never really get to spend much time together at all.

He would obviously make comments about what we were doing. He would drop into the studio here and then when he could, but we never really hung out very much.

He just struck me as the can-do type of person.

We'd discuss things and I could tell that he'd been spending the same considerable amount of time as I had twiddling with knobs and fiddling with a processor and, therefore, had very specific opinions about what techniques to use.

A lot of those struck me as very cutting edge – a very forward-thinking person who's not afraid to take chances.

Yet he would sometimes make it very clear that something shouldn't be polished or try to be too fancy.

He was certainly the man-with-the-plan. He knew what he wanted to get and, in contrast, I think I go into situations differently – "well, I'll just try to feel it out" – almost like I'm an improviser.

In the case of the 'Violator' mix, there were obviously many specifics where it was definitely, "well, this is the vibe we want and that's how we're gonna get it".

He really struck me as someone who was able to articulate that vision so much better than I would ever be able to.

I was in awe of Martin for being the master of being vague. But in Flood's case, he would be able to discuss some technical detail to achieve some details – "well, this is how I do this, this is how I like to do that, and that's why, and this is what I'm trying to achieve with it" – and I just thought I'm really out of my league here.

I like to know how a song feels. Does it have a good vibe? How can I get it to feel better? I have techniques. But generally speaking, like the world that I come from – the world of dance music or jazz – it's really about improvising.

What I always tried to do is utilise the equipment and the tools that are there to illustrate a feeling.

But with Flood, he clearly had much more command of that than I could ever have.

I probably had my own conceptual ideas or ways of approaching things. But he was like that from the moment I met him.

It was very humbling for me to just meet someone and he's not taking 20 minutes to talk about it. He just says, "Okay. It's going to be like this."

That's what I wanted and that's what I did.

I think that's his nature as a producer and that's probably why he's done so well – he really knows exactly what a band needs.

I also think Daniel Miller's role was still very important – being the guiding influence and the great inspirer he can be.

He has many qualities which I think are unsung.

But the incredible talent that Daniel has is that he could just be in the room and not say a thing but yet he'll get you to do what needs to be done!

That is amazing... astonishing.

Obviously, he did express certain opinions that he was thinking – "Well, this could be a bit more like this or that" – but mostly, the way I remember Daniel being was whatever we did, he always managed to make us feel very positive.

Because of their early days together, there's this sort of unspoken chemistry where they're probably so familiar with each other that they don't even need to say anything.

***

Depeche Mode already had an absolutely brilliant record even if I hadn't done a thing to it.

I was obviously trying to bring the songs into focus and frame them in the best possible context, as an entertaining, whole, coherent package.

That goes for each and every song because I believe that each deserves a different treatment.

Yet, you want to make sure that somehow there is something that brings it all together and glues it together.

I always tried to bring out something besides the general feeling of the song.

For some reason, I remember this more specifically in some of the slower songs, spending a great deal of time on 'Blue Dress', 'Clean' or 'Waiting For The Night'.

Sometimes the interludes were really slaved over – how to incorporate them into the way the songs were supposed to go from one to the other.

I also took a keen interest in making sure everything was done for assembling the album master.

I remember sometimes them walking into the control room and saying, "Come on, please. Let's just get this done, already."

You could feel like it was at a level where they weren't quite sure what we may have been doing, or whether it really was worth the extra amount of time I was taking to do this or do that.

I'm sure there were some that we obviously felt might not be the big single contenders and, as such, we went through them maybe a little bit quicker.

I always felt that 'Waiting For the Night' was a terrific track and that it could turn into something really magical – as either a single or in a motion picture or something.

And because of that, I wanted to not only be extremely evocative with the mix but have that classy feel about it that was just something that would blow everyone's minds.

I don't know why, but I always had a bit of a personal preference for 'Waiting For The Night'.

It had an intimacy about Dave's voice and the way the keyboards and the production and everything were done. Even though a lot of Depeche Mode fans are going to think it's the big singles, the big songs that they love, for me, there was something about that particular track that was truly stunning.

It was this sort of abstract, electronic landscape. But yet, it managed to be very emotional, very personal as well.

The song 'Clean' was more about Dave. I felt there was something very dramatic in the lyrics, in the way he was singing it.

I think that probably turned out to be validated a bit later, a few years later when you found out that he, in fact, was going through quite a lot of personal drama.

I could see that he was sometimes having some pretty emotional issues of his own. He would never say much but I could tell that he was really enjoying the way it was going or the way, hopefully, we were trying to use his voice in the mix.

I could tell that when we were mixing it – that there was some sort of struggle, conflict or personal connection with Dave himself and that it should be something that I tried to bring out for the listener to feel.

My interpretation of that was that it should be the same for anyone who was listening to it. It should express a little bit of performance.

***

I was free to make my own schedule, as to when I wanted to work.

And if I didn't feel like working I would just call the assistant and say, "Okay, I'm sorry. I can't come until like later tonight."

I didn't have to explain. Or there would be another time, where I would say, "I want to redo this. Sorry. It was supposed to be my day off but I want to come in."

I did one of the 12-inch versions of 'Enjoy The Silence' that I just wasn't happy with. Nobody questioned any of it.

Someone would just say, "Do whatever you have to do. Just give us a record and however you do it is your business."

As such, given this environment, I think that I took extra care to make sure it was perfect – and that probably is why I came off as slightly pedantic.

But honestly, it's not the way I usually do things.

I tend to gravitate towards the other end of the spectrum, which is to get it done as quickly as possible and capture a vibe that I want and, then, over... finished. Thank you. Let's go home.

But let's not delude ourselves here. The fact that I worked on it or not, I don't think it made any special, incredible difference to it being as well-received as it was.

But there is no question that given the fact that I was hired because I had collaborated with Kraftwerk on a number of things, I felt that part of the reason I was in the project was that they wanted a little bit of that electronic treatment.

And actually, at times, that's what took the time.

***

I remember one funny comment from the people who made the surround sound mix because I wasn't consulted on that.

They said, "Oh, this song. Yeah. We don't know what he did. He had 52 different delays. 52 different types of delays running on one song!"

I even replied to the guys and said, "Hey, have you never heard of this thing called MIDI program change where your delay unit is receiving data through a computer stream and being controlled in real-time so that you can then change the parameters in real-time?"

There were not 52 delays – it's just a couple of delay boxes that keep changing because I kept changing the settings of it live!

I had to program the delay changes using an external computer synchronised to the track. Those would be the kind of things that I felt were certainly my contribution.

I tried to give it as much ear candy and as many really cool things that I felt were appropriate. Not to make it a gimmicky affair at all but to illustrate the music. To give it character.

There's no question that both in the case of the collaboration I did with Kraftwerk as well as Depeche Mode that the electronic side to it was certainly very prominent.

If they had wanted to make a rock album, I was certainly not the person to do it.

Given the songs on the album, the one that struck me immediately as having the most electronic characteristics was certainly 'World In My Eyes'.

It had a real, full electronic approach to it. I even probably did a bit more of that in the 12-inch remixes of it that I did.

But you could say fairly that my contribution to 'Violator' was to give the entire album an overall enhancement of the electronic side of Depeche Mode, rather than maybe the more live, rockier side.

If I was to look back on the rough mixes that were given to me and try to analyse them because even though the mixes were called rough mixes, I'm sure they spent a fair amount of time just presenting it well enough that it came across as something that sort of was coherent.

All the parts were there, all the cool things were there. I just think that I took the extra effort to make them as beautiful and special and intriguing as I knew how to.

I believe that even if I try to, I cannot get rid of the fact that a lot of my sensibility and aesthetics are predicated on an attitude toward electronic and dance music.

I can hear bits in 'Policy Of Truth' or 'Personal Jesus' that I did but which perhaps wouldn't have been done by someone else, such as stripping down a little piece or giving it a little more of a clubby vibe.

I did spend quite a bit of time making sure those details were taken care of.

At times, it required a lot of effort because in those days we didn't have all the facilities that we so much take for granted nowadays – all the computer-controlled devices and pieces of software that do all these treatments.

Back in those days, you kind of had to do it manually or you had to work with someone who invented it.

I remember having an external computer slaved to the tape, so as the tape was running, my computer was also sending the control signals and information and whatever else to the processing units.

***

Flood's style was very raw and direct. He would purposely avoid using reverbs or things that he felt were making the song too smooth.

I guess for me, on the other hand, it was all about finding some interesting combination of lush elements or things that enhanced whatever I thought was an important part of the track – but not necessarily in ways that were so apparent.

In doing that, maybe paying a little bit less attention to the rocky character of the song and paying more attention to the synthetic textures.

For example, we did a mix of 'Enjoy The Silence' in New York that was so abstract and so completely unlike the original.

We passed the vocal through a machine that actually extracted the vocal pitch information and then we got a synthesiser to re-sing it.

I also remember, on the 12-inch, playing the vocal at the same time as a $5 robot toy that had a fluttering sound.

Part of the reason why I was hired is I was obviously one of the people who at that time in those years who are pretty much at the forefront of the electronic music mixing, or one of the few that probably had a foot in the technical end and a foot in the club world that could sort of make sense of it all.

I would imagine, had I not been there, the album might have sounded a little bit different in that respect.

***

I was certainly aware that Dave was going through some personal things. I could tell that he was kind of distraught. It was a bit heavy.

But we were all hanging out, we were doing stuff together and everybody was having a decent time generally, including some fun moments and clowning about.

Sometimes when you work so hard, you also need to let off steam – steam was certainly being let off at regular intervals.

I remember in Milan going to some hard clubs but there was never a sense of debauchery that I so often picked up in other people in similar situations.

I also very clearly remember going to Dingwalls in London and having the time of my life!

But by the time we were in London, we just worked straight – work, work, work, work because we had to get it done.

Sure, when steam needed to be let off, steam was certainly being let off. There's nothing wrong with that.

They'd always be watching football, too. Alan actually took me to see his team, QPR.

We did all the sorts of things that lads do – going to the pub and just having a good time. I just think that's the way they got through that whole period.

They were very down-to-earth and lovely people to be around.

***

The playback was done at the studio as soon as I brought the master tape from the mastering place.

I didn't get much sleep, as I was spending a great deal of time on things by this point.

There were a number of concerns I had about the quality of the mastering and it being really top-notch.

I personally attended the most important sessions once we had all the elements put together – the moment where you take all your master mixes that are in separate reels and separate boxes and you make it become one reel – one box per side.

That involved a lot of tricky stuff because we had these interludes, crossfades and special things that were planned so that as one song fades another start.

It was almost like the apex of my time on 'Violator'. I just wanted to see it through.

I just wanted to make sure that it had the best possible presentation and treatment. So many times in the past, I had things that I felt were really good in the studio but it became weaker by a mastering job that was just careless.

I personally made a safety copy before leaving the mastering room so that I knew no matter what would happen to me, it wouldn't be lost.

But I remember thinking at playback, "Wow, this is incredible. This is really lovely."

I was so proud of what they had done and what we had accomplished together.

I was never privy to what they each thought, except that there were no questions. No one ever asked for anything to be redone, touched up, or changed, or altered, which I was fully prepared to do.

I was expecting something, after working on it for almost a year on and off – in fact, it wouldn't strike me as weird at all if the artist would ask, "Well, can this not be altered?" or, "Can we not make this different?"

Or the producer would say, "Well, it's not quite the way I wanted this transition to work." Or, "Could you roll off a little bit of the mid-range from this part because that's too harsh."

There was none of that. It was just like, "That's it. We did it. It's done."

It was more about raising a toast and celebrating a job well done. That's all I remember. No redos, no edits, no nothing. It was just, bang! Done.

I sometimes ask myself why 'Violator' is so special. I think, first and foremost, it is because of that confluence of songwriting and performance.

All the rest that was done was the icing on the cake – even down to the imagery that Anton picked. It was so strong in its simplicity.

Panos Sialakas (Greece), fan

It's not an easy task thinking back to 1990. I mean, the process of going back 30 whole years can be both nostalgic and painful, especially when I have to remember the very different conditions in the Greek society and the surrounding technology, but also (and mainly) the fragile period of being an oversensitive teenager in the late-1980s / early-1990s.

Under those circumstances, I fell in love with Depeche Mode in the spring of 1989.

It was the time when the media scene in Greece was changing rapidly with the launching of private and satellite stations, including MTV.

And Depeche Mode, as part of a major scene that was happening back then, were one of the bands that I had started to like a lot. There was a certain sense of freedom about their music and a much cooler sense of style than most of the other acts of the time.

And then in the late summer of 1989, 'Personal Jesus' came and stunned me! Here's the latest Depeche Mode record... but not like the Depeche Mode we already knew. For a 15-year-old kid like me, it was something totally new, like I had discovered a new language.

I wouldn't stop listening to the song but most importantly, watching that spaghetti western video of those four cool guys (even Fletch on the rocking horse) over and over again.

One thing I noticed on MTV was the lack of an album being mentioned in the credits. Back then, I couldn't get hold of all the information I have today, and the fact that 'Personal Jesus' had been released less than six months after '101' made me think that it was just a standalone single.

The rest of the year, and the 80s, were passing by with our attention focused on the massive changes in Eastern Europe. The world was changing.

It was changing for me in relation to Depeche Mode too. In early-1990, MTV advertised an exclusive screening premiere of DM's latest single called, 'Enjoy The Silence'. It was Monday morning and I was able to ditch a couple of school hours (sorry, mom and dad) in order to watch it.

About four minutes after that first viewing, I found myself in tears. That was beautiful. I found my favourite band.

And I wasn't alone. Similar to other places around the world, that was when Depeche Mode were becoming a major force in Greece too. They had built a strong reputation with their one-hour performance in July of 1985 at the infamous 'Rock In Athens' festival, and by the time of 'Violator' they had developed a cult following here as well, including the formation of the fan club called Hysterika.

'Personal Jesus' and 'Enjoy The Silence' were played repeatedly on Greek radio. In addition to MTV there were other satellite TV stations at the time – like Super Channel, Sky and RTL – playing the iconic Anton Corbijn videos as well.

Depeche Mode were getting big everywhere and my little country was no exception

As for me, I never looked back after that. Depeche Mode is still my big love. I remember those days very fondly because of them and, believe me, that's not a minor deal for me at all.

They were troubled and confusing times and 'Violator', in particular, was one of the major things I had in order to find the power to deal with the world.

32 years later, it still is.

Chapter 3

Composition Of A Sound

"The thing about working with Depeche Mode is that they're not just professional – they're really smooth and really fun and nice to work with."

***

In May 1989, Dave Gahan, Martin Gore, Alan Wilder, Andy Fletcher, Flood and band assistant Daryl Bamonte left London for Milan to begin recording the follow-up to 'Music For The Masses'.

A six-week stay in the northern Italian city was planned as the first of two main periods of recording, with the finishing touches and mixing scheduled to take place sometime later in the year, in London.

After the first two albums, 'Speak And Spell' and 'A Broken Frame', both of which had been recorded and mixed in the UK capital, Depeche had settled into a regular pattern of taking themselves overseas when it was time to head to the studio.

Although the famous Hansa facility in West Berlin had become the second home of sorts to the band, Daniel Miller and Gareth Jones for 'Construction Time Again', 'Some Great Reward' and 'Black Celebration', a new production regime for 'Music For The Masses' also meant a move to a new city – Paris.

Guillaume Tell Studios, on the western fringes of central Paris, played host to the band in early 1987 as they recorded the majority of the album's tracks, with the remaining sessions taking place at Konk in London.

The mixing for the album and its singles took place mostly at a studio complex, as Gahan would describe it, "in the middle of nowhere", known as Puk – an extremely rural facility about 40 miles from the northern Danish city of Aarhus.

Despite its remoteness, Puk was a studio that the band had enjoyed being in and, more importantly for those with one eye on the schedule, where they were able to knuckle down and work hard, rather than be distracted from the obvious temptations of a big city, such as Berlin, Paris or even London, which was close to where the four band members still lived.

Puk was therefore booked for the second round of recording sessions in the late summer of 1989, but first up was a month-and-a-half in Milan, at Logic Studios.

This strategy suited the band's desire at the time to make sure they were able to enjoy their time recording a new album, not least because despite being almost a decade into their career, they and their new producer were all still under the age of 30 and were well known, from previous projects, for their capacity to party at the same time as approaching the more serious work of laying down tracks for a new record.

Milan seemed like an obvious choice. It had a lively club scene and was close enough by air to London for the inevitable visits home for the band, and also for those coming in from Mute Records.

Most importantly, it was home to Logic, a studio that had been getting a name for itself in production circles as a first-rate facility following its creation in the mid-1980s by Carmelo and Michelangelo La Bionda.

The Italian brothers were credited with being the part of the movement behind the formation of Italo Disco in the early-1980s, a genre that some argue was an influence on a variety of well-known bands from the UK, such as the more up-tempo numbers from the likes of the Pet Shop Boys, New Order and Erasure.

The combination of the La Biondas and their background in pioneering the Italo Disco scene was, of course, not the reason for Flood and the band's decision to use the studio – but rather its equipment, location, staff and atmosphere.

***

As early as nine months before recording began, just weeks after the Pasadena Rose Bowl gig, Depeche Mode were weighing up how they would approach the album, already conscious of the fact that they had decided that they would want to do so in a different way to previous records.

Flood was already pushing for a massive change in how the band would get ready for the first recording session in Italy in the spring of 1989.

Compared to previous years, where the band and their production team would sit down and decide on the style, feel, methods to be used and the general direction that the record would take, Flood argued for a radically new approach.

It may not have been drastically different for many other bands, but it was a fundamentally unusual process for a band that had previously arrived in the studio with a strategy and, most crucially, Gore's songs in demo form at a reasonably advanced stage.

Instead, Flood – with the rest of the band's support, especially Wilder – insisted to Gore that his demos were presented as simply as possible: vocal melody, verses and chorus, and maybe a basic chord structure.

Even the tempo of the songs, as the production team and the band would later discover, was to be left open to possible reinterpretation or, indeed, wholesale alteration once they were entrenched in the studio.

To Gore this was a massive surrender of his usual creative process given his earlier, fully-baked demos would often sound reasonably close to the final recorded outcome. More importantly, he was putting an enormous amount of faith in his bandmates and Flood, the producer that the band had never worked with in the studio.

Still, Gore realised that a change needed to be made if they were to fulfil the ambition of taking the Depeche Mode sound in a new, different and exciting direction.

Part of that relinquishing of relative power over the final output was eased with the support and urging of the band, primarily because they realised their songwriter had given birth to a collection of lyrics and melodies that had arguably surpassed any of his previous creations.

Talking to 'Select' magazine in 1990, Gore said "In the past, I'd always demoed the songs at home and presented them to the band in quite finished form. By that stage your ideas are pretty fixed, so we had tended to simply copy the demos, to make them better.

"But this time the band asked me to keep the songs as basic as I could. Sometimes it would just be guitar and vocal, or organ and vocal.

"We had no preconceptions and we didn't spend any time on pre-production, where we'd usually spent, say, six weeks in a programming suite working things out. This time we took these very basic songs into the studio and tried to do it very spontaneously."

Wilder continues the theme, albeit in his slightly more pointed style, in an interview with the 'NME' the same year, "We were beginning to have a problem with boredom in that we felt we'd reached a certain level of achievement in doing things in a certain way."

***

There was a degree of trepidation that they were all heading back into the studio, as a unit, after such a long time.

Firstly, it was the most extended period in the band's career that they had been away from one another.

Although the band had officially been on a break since the 'Music For The Masses' tour had ended with that famous summer evening in Pasadena in the summer of 1988, inevitably there was plenty of activity around the release of the '101' package of a movie, double album and live version of 'Everything Counts' in late 1988 and early 1989.

Promotional work for '101' was a wholly different environment to the creative process required for working on Gore's new songs, with a new producer and studio team.

The main body of recording work that took place in the spring and summer of 1989 was conducted in two very different environments: the party town of Milan, with the engineers Pino Piscotola and Roberto Baldi for the intensive early work; and the quiet, almost serene and secluded Puk studio in the Danish countryside.

If Logic in Milan set the scene for the process and creativity, alongside plenty of visits to Milan's famous nightlife scene at the time, Puk had a far more laid-back living and work ethic.

The on-site pool and gardens were in stark contrast to the urban setting of Logic, giving the band time and space to refine their initial creations and begin to hone what would become the 'Violator' sound.

"We wanted to take a different direction with this album," Gahan said during a filmed interview for Swedish television that took place by the pool at Puk. "We wanted the songs to come across in a more direct way and not to be so fussy, to try and get a lot more energy on to tape when we're recording, rather than play around with sounds for so long that by the time you get around to record you've forgotten about the direction of the song."

The band wanted to work a lot faster than on previous long-players but, as Gahan admitted, they had ended up taking longer because they were experimenting more.

The result was a lot harder, yet not in a rocky way – that would come later with some of the tracks on the 'Songs Of Faith And Devotion' album in 1993 – with an overall edgy sound.

The change in the creative process, production and eventual sound of the new Depeche Mode were fermented in Milan and taken through to the Puk sessions, with a conscious effort made to dispel the 'doomy' label that had been levelled at the band over the previous four albums.

No longer were computers and electronics the sole providers of the heartbeat and emotion of a song. Instead, the band had introduced some live elements such as percussion and guitars to give additional 'feeling' to each track and what Gahan believed was a new, emotive Depeche Mode.

What hadn't changed from previous recording processes was the band's headstrong belief that the music that they make is for themselves, rather than figure out how to create a song that will be a hit.

If they could do the latter they would be "very successful", Gahan joked, somewhat playing down, in the typically ironic tone of so many of their interviews, the considerable success they had already achieved until that point.

At the heart of what the band was doing during the recording sessions was pushing their creativity, while retaining the identity of Depeche Mode – to take the process and the ideas further than before.

The word "risk" was used on many occasions during interviews to promote 'Violator'. Its use indicated just how much the

Logic and Puk sessions had challenged preconceived thinking about their ideas and the sound of the record.

Fans and the critics who later praised 'Violator' would inevitably say that the risk-taking was worth the effort, yet it was clearly a method that was still in its nascent phase for the band.

The result was that the recording sessions took time and the band agonised over everything being right – they were, increasingly, becoming "a lot more precious", as Gahan put it at the time, about the final body of work.

Depeche Mode had always poured as much of their emotional energy, production prowess and ideas into each album as they could.However, the inherent risks that they had taken with 'Violator' during the two main recording sessions in Italy and Denmark had created something that would both surprise and delight those who were about to hear the first fruits of their efforts.

They had always wanted to make the perfect record. This time, without question, they had it.

***

The relative calm of Puk was soon over and the band found themselves combining the process of promoting the upcoming first single 'Personal Jesus' with finishing the album.

François Kevorkian's mixing work on the track – marrying its rockier sensibilities with an electronic edge – ensured he was kept on for the remainder of the album, as and when finished tracks were made available for him to work on from his Axis studio in New York City.

At this stage, engineer Steve Lyon was brought in to work on some tracks recorded at Dave Stewart's Church Studios in London and a fairly frantic period took over.

Kevorkian was working hard on the mixes from finished tracks and ideas were being thrown around about how to finish what would be the second single, 'Enjoy The Silence'.

The song had completely metamorphosed during the sessions in Denmark, leading to disagreements and a degree of nervousness over what was already anticipated to be one of the most popular tracks in the band's history.

The ballad-like demo had become, in Gore's words, "a disco track" courtesy of Flood and Alan Wilder's overhaul. In its new guise, Depeche Mode knew they had a hit on their hands and the likes of Mute supremo Daniel Miller – with his experience in production and the music business – had specific ideas of how the song should sound.

A compromise was eventually found, with Miller's ideas being used for the single release in early 1990 and a tweaked representation finding its way to the rendition used for the album.

Although Miller was not directly involved in much of the session work for 'Violator', such was the respect and father-like presence he still had with the band that he was allowed to stamp his mark on such an important song.

By the autumn of 1989, 'Violator' was finished bar the creation of the remixes that would eventually adorn every single release over the course of the next year.

A dizzying array of producers and mixers were enlisted to tinker with 'Enjoy The Silence', including the band's friend and former studio comrade Gareth Jones, as well as the return of Bomb The Bass' Tim Simenon (who would later work on Depeche Mode's 1997 album 'Ultra' and On-U Sound's Adrian Sherwood.

Kevorkian himself would create several remixes of 'World In My Eyes' and 'Policy Of Truth', pushing both into territories that maintained their original framework but had elements of house music thrown in. They became some of the most popular remixes the band ever released.

Alongside the album tracks, Depeche Mode also produced three B-sides during the recording sessions that many consider being some of their best, and which could have potentially been songs included on the album itself – 'Dangerous', 'Happiest Girl', 'Sea Of Sin' and the instrumental 'Kaleid'.

Pino Pischetola (Italy), engineer on 'Violator' at Logic Studio in Milan

Logic Studio in Milan, at the time, was the best studio in Italy.

The La Bionda brothers, who were singers and producers, used their money to build this studio.

It was really well designed by an English studio designer called Andy Munro, who was probably one of the best in the world.

Like everybody in my field, you started as an assistant and then you move to be an engineer and then you become a recording engineer and so on.

So there was a project by an Italian artist that was produced by Alan Moulder, and I assisted him as the in-house engineer.

And so when I asked Flood, "How come you chose this studio and me as an engineer?". He said because he knew Alan Moulder had been working in the studio and that he said it was very professional, that he really liked it and then he recommended me.

So this is how I got involved!

The idea was to split the recording into two different parts, with the first one being in the city and the other part in Denmark, in a middle of nowhere kind of place known as Puk.

It was perhaps to have two different kinds of atmospheres. So they booked our studio for six weeks.

I think they probably wanted to use the first session to get the musical direction for the record.

And so that's why they wanted to finish 'Personal Jesus' because they wanted to know if François Kevorkian was the right choice for mixing the entire album.

Daniel Miller is a huge fan of Kraftwerk and he wanted to see if François could also enter the 'Violator' project. In a way, Flood was enough but they also wanted to take it one more step ahead.

François was really part of the Kraftwerk sound at that time, so he was the perfect person to get involved.

Still, I remember the truck bringing the equipment, all the synthesisers and stuff. And although the control room was quite big, they filled it up with all kinds of instruments.

For me, it was really challenging because I didn't have a lot of experience in the studio, so I was a bit scared.

***

When you are an engineer, if you are dealing with a producer from a background of songwriting – I'm not saying you can fool them – but they don't notice every turn of a knob.

But when it's Flood, who is probably one of the best in the world, every move you make you really need to be conscious about it.

So the prospect of working with everybody, with the band, with Flood, was very intimidating.

I first met Flood literally when they were hooking up all the instruments.

After two or three days I asked him how I was doing and he said, "You're doing good, otherwise after ten minutes I would have asked you to stick around just for getting the coffee.

"It's a very important project for me and I can't risk using somebody who isn't up to the level, otherwise it would put the project in danger."

His attention to detail was amazing.

When he came in, he noticed a slight difference in the sound of the two control room speakers. I was really impressed. Wow, what an ear!

Or when he was choosing a microphone for things, he would try out four or five mics of the same model and choose the one he thought sounded best for that particular bit.

He was also very quiet, hardworking but comfortable to work with. He would never create tension. He would just work until something was right.

He would do this by saying "We have to make a great record and to make a great record, we need a lot of hard work, and we have to do it".

In the end, it's very simple, even if the process sounds so complicated.

Because they were professionals, nobody wanted to say, "No, I prefer to go out clubbing, I don't care about this right now".

***

The band were always very nice to me, but one little problem was the language. They speak English with a strange accent – unusual for an Italian to listen to!

We usually got people from London or New York or from LA, but their English was a bit difficult to understand and they were using some difficult words, too.

Sometimes I wouldn't understand some things so they had a bit of fun with it. They often used slang-like terms. This wasn't a problem for them, but it was a reason to have a bit of a laugh with me.

***

The first thing that happened was that Martin wanted to set up in another studio in the building. He wanted a sampling area where he could make sounds from scratch.

In fact, one thing that surprised me was that they never appeared to use a sound twice.

They had a huge library of great sounds but, as a rule, every sound had to be created from scratch each time.

This really impressed me because it would be quicker and easier to use pre-created sounds.

The demos did represent the songs but in a basic arrangement. The vocals were only performed by Martin, too.

Martin used to play this 12-track AKAI machine that was a tape recorder and mixer. It was very modern for the time because the only way to record was on big tapes which were huge – yet this was almost portable.

It wasn't portable as we think of it now, but you could put it in a flight case, so it was in the studio in Milan. It was something you could easily lift and move. The melodies and rhythms were there but obviously, a lot of work was still to be done in the studio.

So the process in the studio was divided between assigning sounds to rhythm parts that were already in the demo and assigning guitar and vocals and everything else.

Dave was not involved until later on when the tracks were made ready to record vocals on. But he was certainly involved, making comments about songs during meetings in the studio.

We wanted to work song-by-song, to give each a basic structure and then move on to the next.

Then in the evenings, we would do dubs on different songs, such as vocals or guitar.

What impressed me was the schedule – it was really precise. We started at 11 or 12 in the morning and finished at midnight. At 7 pm we always went for dinner, and it stayed the same for six weeks. They were really on it, professionally.

There was not one single day where they have been clubbing at night and didn't show up for work in the morning.

This surprised me, because sometimes, especially in Italy, people are really flexible with schedules in the studio. Maybe they show up in the afternoon, maybe they don't show up or maybe they show up early. It's not a precise way of working.

There was a drum kit and a few amplifiers, where they would play rock songs after they had finished recording and before they would go for dinner or go out at night.

But during the working day, there was always a big focus on the project.

From what I can tell, they were never on drugs or alcohol. They were really clean in the studio, all the time.

There wasn't a sort of, "Let's get stoned and see what comes out musically" mentality, never.

It was really almost military.

***

Every sound was meticulously found and worked on and when it was ready, we would print it on tape and move on to the next part.

In this process, it was mainly Alan and Flood doing the sound programming and such. Martin said that his work was done, so now it was their turn.

It was natural that this is how their relationship started, too – Alan and Flood.

The man to work with Flood was more into sound and programming – and because Martin was into sampling and he had his own studio, he was less involved.

It was like "Okay, you do your work and we will talk about it later". Of course, they liked it and where it was going, so from then on it was actually like a well-oiled engine.

A big example of this is the stomp rhythm for 'Personal Jesus'.

It was amazing because they recorded all kinds of stomping on different surfaces – the flat, studio floor, cases, and the staircase of the building.

We had 30 metres of cables and put microphones on the staircase and recorded them there.

Then everything was sampled and played with the keyboard to get the rhythm really tight.

It was a completely acoustic sound, with different kinds of sources - but they still played it all together at the same time, many different stomping noises all put together in this perfect rhythm.

It was hard work but a lot of fun, professionally. I was doing a lot of things that I never imagined I would be doing!

Another thing was the rule not to re-use parts, in a way.

Keyboard sounds can be monophonic or parts, like with chords where fingers are playing three different notes.

A lot of their music consisted of monophonic parts that worked together.

In fact, it's difficult to find a lot of chords, strings or keyboard sounds in their songs.

So what we had to do was get all these monophonic sounds and stick them together.

***

Depeche Mode weren't really into, "I like this song" or "I don't like this bit". They considered the whole picture.

Certainly, for 'Violator', I think it was normal to suggest and change things. It wasn't a problem - it's just that a song can be made in many different ways.

Since we had so many instruments and sounds and so many ways of doing things, the result could be very different depending on what we would choose.

But what was interesting was the involvement of Andy Fletcher. It was really important because if it wasn't working technically, his opinion or his judgement of the work was really important.

There are some producers, like Rick Rubin – he doesn't play an instrument, he just sits on the couch but his opinions are somehow more important than that of a working producer.

So there were a lot of meetings in the studio, with just the four of them, because they had this thing where they were their own management.

When a band is this huge, there has to be a way of knowing and trusting people, and so during these meetings, each opinion was very important.

It was Fletch's job to organise the release campaigns, radio contracts and all such managerial tasks. They were constantly all talking about these things.

I remember one occasion when he came back from England and he had over 1,000 postcards to sign – so every bit of time off they had, it was signing postcards...forever!

But it was a sign that they still wanted a great relationship with their fans.

***

Normally, to record the vocals the singer goes into the booth and uses the best microphone the studio has.

But the vocals for 'Violator' in Milan were all done in the control room, with the speakers quite loud and certainly not the most expensive microphone!

Technically, this is very difficult to do. The leakage of the speakers to the microphones can be really dangerous.

Dave has a really powerful voice, so if you keep the mic really close to your mouth, to have a proper volume, you can turn down the volume on the pre-amp so the gain of the mic isn't that high and, then, it doesn't pick up everything else.

Also, with compression, when you sing, the gained structure of the signal goes down because the compressor pushes down the sound.

So all the leakage from the speaker is pushed down as well. As soon as you clean the vocals in the mix, between the phrases, the leakage during the singing is really quiet.

If you do not have a powerful voice, you can't do this.

This was the great thing about Flood. Not many producers would be so open-minded to say, "I'm looking for the best performance. I don't care if the sound isn't great".

The performance had to be great.

They would still make two or three good takes for a vocal and then select the best one for each line of the song.

This was mainly Flood working with Dave.

***

'Personal Jesus' was planned to be released long before the album, so they needed to finish it – recording and mixing – much earlier.

This was also a good reason to try working with François – to see if it would also work for the whole album.

I can see now that it was also a test to see if the overall set-up was good and if it was going to work. Was Flood the best producer at the time? Was François the best person to mix the track?

But during the mixing of 'Personal Jesus', the band and Flood were not even in the studio.

They moved to another studio to do the B-side, 'Dangerous', and moved most of the equipment for five days, so they left François alone, just to see what he was able to achieve with that one song.

But halfway through the mix, François wanted to overdub some parts with some ideas he had about rhythmic parts and some keyboards.

So Alan came back to the studio for a couple of nights to do these overdubs. But other than that, it was just François, an American engineer [Dennis Mitchell] and then me.

François, like Flood, was really on another planet. Flood was more like a producer. He didn't touch the desk very often – he just wanted to sit down and listen.

With François, once his engineer had set up the song, he did it all by himself on the desk.

As an engineer myself, it was really great to watch – the way he was using effects, EQ and compressions.

Even before the mix, we'd all worked very hard on the track.

I don't think the guitar riff was there on the demo – or if it was, it was not so important. The riff was really developed as a big sound in the studio.

In fact, both the acoustic guitar and electric guitar took quite some time to do.

The rhythm was already in the demo, but not the footsteps. But all the parts were from Martin's computer – a BBC computer.

The great thing was that it had four media ports – and each port was independent, so the timing of the notes was very tight and precise.

If you produce a lot of notes, it becomes very sloppy because it is a serial protocol. It sends out one note at a time.

So, if in a part there are eight notes, from the first one to the last one, there are a few milliseconds of difference in time – and this makes the song not very tight.

Instead, if you have four ports, the four notes come out at the same time. Because their music was about tightness, if it was not precise, it didn't work.

The track was eventually on 48 tracks, which was a lot at that time.

The studio had two 24-track machines that were running in sync, so you could use all 48 tracks.

But this was helpful as we did lots of mixes!

In the album version, if you listen to the song, after three and a half minutes, it changes completely. It becomes more Kraftwerk, more electronic.

That was all François' work and Alan's. He wanted Alan to come back in the studio for a few nights, to edit and play the parts in the song – more like a programmer with the music.

He wanted Alan also to use Depeche Mode sounds and not do it by himself. Plus Alan is a great keyboard player.

During another mix of 'Personal Jesus', I remember François listened to it many times and then he had this idea to put American-style preachers as a sample. That's what became "The Lord Jesus Christ himself" sample.

In order to get that, François called a friend in Los Angeles that had a recording of everything you might want. So he calls him late at night and says, "Listen, I need something very quick. Something with preachers speaking."

And his friend says, "Okay. I will FedEx it to you in a couple of hours." So two days later, using what must have used the fastest courier in the world – super extra express or something – we got a cassette from LA with all the preachers on it.

We spent two hours listening to all the preachers and different phrases, and then François picked up on that one and a few others to put into a sampler and fly in the song at a certain moment. That was really a fun thing to do.

Another remarkable thing he did was the reverse effect before the, "Reach out and touch faith!" lyric. You get a sound like, "Ahhhhh".

It's the vocals, in reverse – an effect you do in the studio.

If you put reverb in after a sound, the sound of the reverb always decays. It's very dense in the beginning and then it decays.

If you record the reverb and then put the tape in the right direction, the reverb comes earlier and increases in volume. So that was his idea.

To do that now, with products and plug-ins in the studio, you can do in three seconds. At that time, it was a really difficult thing to do.

Also, there was no undo button. Now, if you make a mistake you can press undo and go back to where it was before.

At the time, it just wasn't possible. When we were doing the mixes, in order to create empty tracks to put new ideas in the song, we had to premix some parts into a stereo mix, so maybe eight tracks would become two.

And then those two would free up six tracks to put on other parts. Nowadays you have hundreds. At that time, it was not possible.

Some nights, François would go to the hotel, saying: "Okay, you now free up some tracks. I will see you tomorrow."

And so doing one of these bounces, me and the engineer accidentally erased the main guitar riff.

I went to a studio in the building, at 2 am, took an AKAI sampler, sampled the guitar from another part of the song and then went back to the beginning and threw the recorded part into the erased position.

And at the time we did it maybe four or five times and then we got it right. And then it was back to normal!

It was a secret until now.

***

The mixing of the extended version of 'Personal Jesus' – the Pump Mix – was already at 29 hours in the studio. I was almost dead but we had to finish it.

The problem was that François had to leave for Japan. He already had a session booked there and he had a tight schedule and couldn't miss it.

But on the Friday morning that he was going to leave, so we started the remix and the remix goes with this process of doing piece by piece – adding parts, adding samples, two different versions of the same part of the song, muting instruments, doing crazy effects and stuff.

And this never stops. By the time Dennis had left that studio, it was only me and François. The hours are creeping up. The band were working on 'Dangerous' in the other studio, so we carried on.

And so on the morning of the last day, the taxi was outside the studio waiting for him.

But François listens to the tape and says: "You know what – it needs another thirty seconds."

It was already six minutes long.

He was so professional, that he cancelled his flight to do the next 30 seconds of music. I said, "No problem. I am not dying, I'm doing it."

So we worked all morning to do these thirty seconds. He had to catch another plane in the afternoon.

So, later, the band comes into the studio with Flood, to listen to the extended mix - but François has already left.

They listened to it and obviously, they really liked it. But someone, I don't know if it was Martin, Flood or I don't remember who it was, said: "It's beautiful, but it's a bit long!"

So I explained to them that to make it longer, François had to cancel his fight and everything. So out of respect, they left it as it was and didn't cut it...

***

I always remember the 'Personal Jesus' playback.

They all came in together, before going back into the studio. The single version was almost finished. And then we were supposed to go off and do the remix version.

But already in the single version, there was the reverse, all the overdubs that Alan did.

But I remembered that they loved it. Flood as well.

Daniel Miller also came to Milan and he took the tapes to England, to transfer to vinyl – the mastering.

I think he did it in every studio in London. Because two or three days later, he came back to Milan and he had five or six 12-inch vinyl, each made in a different studio.

So we brought a turntable into the studio and listened to all of them.

It was a blind listen because sometimes the name can influence you and they sounded really different from one another because in mastering you can change the sound a lot.

So the band and Flood chose the best sounding one and that became the master.

Even today, I don't know many songs that sound like 'Personal Jesus', in any way. From the lyrics to the melody to the arrangement. It was really something new.

You have to remember that this project came quickly after '101'. And so for them, it was like, "We can make it really big in the States this time".

But there was a necessity to do something new... not relax.

Music is a really strange thing and it isn't mathematics.

Things that make a great record are so many and yet so delicate - the balance is also really difficult to get, which is why when you get it, it's great.

When you perform a song, it's nothing – it's nothing compared to a record following the things that are done in production.

Music speaks for itself. When you listen to a song, if you are an experienced musician or artist you know when something is elite or not.

With 'Violator', after a few days of putting down a few ideas, we knew 'Personal Jesus' was already a huge step in thinking, "Yes, we are doing a great job here".

***

'Personal Jesus' was a very strong and brave thing to do.

Talking about Italy, where religion is something so big, we have the Vatican a few hours or so from Milan. But here it was played a lot, probably because no one understood what they were saying!

When we were in the studio, Anton came in and did the photoshoot for the cover with the naked girl.

And the video was also a new thing. Not at the same level as 'Enjoy The Silence', whose video was another new step in video making, but 'Personal Jesus' was, well, risque.

They knew it though. They would talk a lot about this thing, about the fact that their target is not the usual Depeche Mode target. It was something bigger. And a new sound.

For example, if you listen to U2 records, the experimental stuff was two years after 'Violator'. And Flood at the time was starting to work with Nine Inch Nails, but they were still like a heavy metal band with electronics.

They were not as experimental as they became afterwards.

So 'Violator' was probably the first big electronic, experimental record. To sound in a new way, using samples and new sounds and a mixture of acoustic sounds processed in such a way that they are not recognisable.

I think it was the first big record made like this.

Steve Lyon (UK), engineer on 'Violator' at The Church Studios in London

Someone I knew was working with Dave Stewart and Annie Lennox at the Eurythmics studio in Crouch End, so I became the engineer there.

I was freelancing, doing other things in London, but then the management of the studio rang up and said, "You know this band called Depeche Mode are coming?"

I knew them, but I was completely unaware of their recent background. I'd heard some of the stuff from 'Black Celebration' and 'Music For The Masses', but it never really bit into me.

I'd been trained by a producer called John Jones and I was doing some stuff for him as well.

But then they rang a second time and said, "Steve, I really think you should do this – we really need someone... they want someone with that kind of experience."

So I went over and met Alan Wilder and Flood, initially, and then the rest of the guys.

I knew Flood from his work with U2 and Nick Cave, but I still thought, "Okay, but I've never really done a record like this before and I'd never done this kind of thing because I was very much like a band person."

They were all electronics, there was no live playing obviously... it seemed much more limited than I was used to.

There was a lot of sampling and I'd never really got the grips with it before, so I was very upfront with them and said, "Well look, what I do really is this stuff but I'm happy to learn."

They said, "Don't worry, it's fine – what we want you to do is just be in the studio all the time and just help us out and do vocals."

Then it was the weekend and they gave me a sampler and said, "Right, take this home, here's the manual, learn how to use it."

They also gave me a copy of 'Personal Jesus' and all the remixes that François Kevorkian had done and I was completely blown away.

"This is incredible," I thought. "This really, really is great." I'd never heard an electronic record produced in that way, with so much power and emotion.

My whole mindset toward them had kind of changed. "Wow, this is fucking incredible – I really, really want to be involved."

Not that I was indifferent to them at all, but I realised that this really was something special.

***

Initially, I was fiddling around a lot with vocals, such as on 'Waiting For The Night'.

We had a 15-80 delay unit – it's kind of old school but it was the bee's knees at the time – and you could sample in it.

I was playing with the distortion on the desk and the delay and the sampler, and I was like, "What about this?" There's a sort of backwards delay that happens in the song and that was us... me and Flood and Alan, just fiddling around.

By then, Alan was very central to what was going on, so I quickly struck up a very good friendship and working relationship with him.

I was really interested in the way he worked, because that was the first time I'd seen that kind of technique before, and he was very interested in my way of working.

I was very much hands-on and liked messing around with sounds and then sending sounds out into the live area.

We had a B3 Hammond organ and some guitar amps and bits and pieces and I would be working alongside Alan with the effects.

On 'Blue Dress', for example, Martin was using a hand-held mic in the control room and the vocals were really good. So we got a BK-800 series mic, which is a very nice mic, and just recorded it there.

The experimentation was great fun.

They had already worked with some really good engineers on 'Violator' – Peter Iversen at Puk and the guys in Milan.

My role was definitely and rightly so, just engineering, but I'd often say, "What about this?" and "Let's do this...".

I remember helping set up the gear downstairs for François Kevorkian – there was a discussion that they had spent a lot of money on hiring equipment for the mixing!

***

By the time they got to London, 'Personal Jesus' was completely finished.

For the other songs, in terms of percentages, it would be anything from 20% to 65-70%, depending on the song.

'Sea Of Sin', for example, which I ended up mixing in an upstairs studio, had had a lot of work done on it, but we were constantly working on the tracks, tweaking them and trying different things.

The riff on 'Policy Of Truth', I remember Alan coming up with that there.

We spent a day on the sampler with the guitar solo. Martin played it, but it was now a backwards sample. It just kind of worked out – Alan was really good at that sort of thing. He'd pick up on something and have a vision for it.

Another was the drumming on 'Halo'. Alan was playing and there also was the drum sample on top of it – I'm not sure if it was the first time but it was certainly a new thing for them: they were doing a drumming session!

For me it was, "Brilliant, we are going to record some drums!" because that's what I do. There were mics everywhere, so that was that and it ended up being the rock track that is 'Halo'.

It was interesting to see how much they wanted to push things.

There's a certain dynamic when you begin a fresh working relationship with people that have obviously worked together on the material previously – in that, Flood had done some remixes for the band and had learned where the boundaries are and what they didn't want to do. However, I would say that in London, the three of us – Flood, Alan and myself – were definitely pushing on. edging towards a rockier record using electronics.

I had been a little afraid of it before but by this time it was, "I don't give a shit."

Flood was driving this, but I think it was a general mood.

***

Dave, Martin and Andy were around all the time. We'd be working on something and Dave would have an idea or an opinion about something and Fletch would as well, and so would Martin.

But the core element driving the sound, by then, was Alan and Flood.

Yet the thing that makes a band really tick is the differences – if everyone was on the same curve then you would have the same all the time.

Fletch was more attentive and would say things like, "Oh we've had a lot of success, let's not shoot ourselves in the foot by doing something that's completely different to what we've done before".

But in all the experimentation and different things that were happening at the time, they had a lot of support from Daniel Miller.

That can only be applauded because it's very difficult for a band with a lot of success to make another record – and one that is very different.

Undoubtedly there were voices within the camp that were saying, "Oh, that might be a bit too much – is it too far away from what we've done?".

I would say that, and only for the right reasons, Fletch was one of those.

Martin is such a great songwriter and he'd done the demos. He was initially kind of reticent, I think, but Dave was definitely, "Let's try to make it a bit rockier".

Let's face it, even the 'Music For The Masses' tour was a rock concert – it's not an electronic band on stage at all.

It was very brave because they'd had a lot of success in the States – they were very well known for a particular type of thing and then they just decided that that didn't really matter anymore.

***

François Kevorkian is an ultra-clean kind of mixer – that's what he does.

The tracks before François mixed them – and he mixed them very well in the end – were slightly more robust and rocky.

I remember the three of us – me at the helm and then Flood and Alan telling me what to do on the desk – we did some rough mixes of the album. They were definitely rockier than the final version of 'Violator'.

'Policy Of Truth', for example, starts with a clean kind of guitar riff. It's just in its nature of electronic sounds to be quite clean.

When we were working on it in the studio it definitely had a bit more of a real drum feel to it and a dirtier sound.

'Halo', which is the rockiest song on the record, too, sounded a bit more like a band – more live.

But I think that is François' thing – he is very good at being clean, crisp, and very precise.

Those mixes he did, though, stood the test of time, without a doubt. You can play them against any track in a club – particularly the new mastered versions – and blow everyone away.

***

Alan had just bought a house in Sussex, so he was doing it up and commuting backwards and forwards to the studio.

Martin was living in London at the time and I remember going round to his house for his birthday.

We went out a few times but we didn't really go out clubbing in London.

It was different from the Milan session – but it was a very social environment at the studio, very positive and friendly.

I love the studio anyway but it was a pleasure walking in the morning and thinking, "Ooh, what are we going to do today?", just because the songs were just so great, you really had a passion to want to work on it.

I was witness to a conversation with Anton about the cover when he came in with it.

It was cool, people would come in with ideas, and then someone else would come in with other ideas about it.

But they weren't the type of band to go, "You should leave the room now because this has nothing to do with you."

You could just courteously stand at the back of the room and kind of watch as they go "Oh, you know, I like that."

But everyone loved the cover – they all thought it was wicked.

There was a sense of relief when the music really started coming together.

But then it was, like, "What comes next? What are we going to do next? What's the next challenge?"

They were not really a band to dwell on stuff. They didn't go around patting themselves on the back.

***

I remember the talk at some point turned to the tour and putting the backing tracks together.

"What are you doing over Christmas?", someone asked.

I didn't really know, so they said, "Well, you've got to come with us upstairs and help put the stuff together for the tour". Pretty much like that!

They used to use a 16-track machine for each song.

To make it easy, you would always have the bass drum for each song on track one, the snare drum on track two, etc.

Obviously, it was a little bit easier with the stuff that they'd already done before, on previous tours.

The 'Violator' stuff I knew pretty well by then, so we set up a pair of big speakers and Alan would say, "Alright, so Fletch is going to play this part, I'm going to do this, Martin is going to do this."

"The sequencer part from 'Enjoy The Silence' – that needs to be on there. The guitar part – Martin is going to play that live. The bass part bit in the middle I'm going to play."

Alan would have the sampler at the back of the room, deciding all the various parts that needed putting down.

All the bits that the band would not be playing live would go on the tape machine – things like the stomp from 'Personal Jesus' or the fireworks from 'Stripped', the bits are so inherent to the sound of the songs.

We also had to fill the sound carefully as well. You obviously couldn't get a bunch of guitars and try to replicate it – it's not Pearl Jam!

We'd have to balance it carefully, thinking we're in a 10,000-person seat arena.

With Depeche it was quite a different set-up to a normal live act – the sounds are so crucial to the vibe, such as the keyboard line at the beginning of 'World In My Eyes'.

I'd never done anything like that before, so I just got a big sub-bass unit, two massive speakers – then I'd turn it up loud and just walk between the songs, thinking, "That needs a bit more bass and this needs a little bit more of something else."

There was a lot of work put into it because it wasn't just, "This was the song, this is the structure."

For example, the intro: 'Kaleid'.

We took a bit from 'Enjoy The Silence', one of the remixes, and then Alan and I did a version together and used that. There was a lot of thought put into it.

The whole thing took a good couple of months.

***

I've been very fortunate in that this has happened a couple of times in my career, but it certainly happened with 'Violator'.

It's when you sit back, listen to a record and think to yourself, "You know what, we've really nailed something here, we've really done something that we can all feel really proud of – it's been a lot of hard work but it's really fucking good."

For us, this wasn't just some macho, "Oh, aren't we great?", but recognition across the board that everyone was really pleased.

We'd also worked so hard, the band had worked hard and, of course, Martin – writing those amazing songs before they even got to record them.

In London, the pressure was on them, which I was oblivious to at the beginning but obviously very aware of by the time we'd finished.

There will always be leaders and certain people do different jobs really well.

Fletch has his role and he does that really well. Martin is one of the best songwriters that this country has ever produced.

Dave is an incredible frontman – head above most of the frontmen that have come out in the last few decades.

But Alan was so intrinsically involved in the production of it, perhaps more so than any of their other previous albums.

He is really good at taking what are already good songs and then making them exceptional.

That is a role that takes a lot of pressure, takes a lot of time and sometimes some of that work is unseen.

You knock around a studio for 24 hours, when you are developing something, and then you play it back to other people in the band and they'll start scratching their heads.

I don't think that the band or the label ever underestimated Alan's role, but I do sometimes think that the work he did went unnoticed.

Phil Legg (UK), engineer on 'Violator' at The Church Studios in London

My story really goes back to 1978, when I came to London from Dorset, joined the band Essential Logic and did a lot of gigs with Daniel Miller.

He and I became friends and I'd manage the Mute studio and move into that when Essential Logic was dead. We did the punk group Marine Girls album, stuff like that, and I was always bumping into Daniel.

I would say, "Yeah I'm doing this, I'm doing that," and we sort of became a bit of a studio team and we would then often mix tracks together. Then I became a sort of high-tech sound engineer. I worked with Power Puff Studios, Robert Miller Studios, and what used to be Morgan studios. Daniel suggested me for Erasure and I worked with Flood as well.

And then the Depeche album was being done and Daniel wasn't happy with 'Enjoy The Silence'. Anyway, Daniel and I went in and just got on with it.

I think Daniel fell in love with the demo and felt like the mix just didn't have that kind of quality. So based on that, Daniel came to me.

We were a bit of a mixing team at the time and we were doing things most weekends. During the week Daniel was doing stuff and I was working on albums, so on our weekends we would get together and mix tracks.

I don't know whether I heard the mixes that Daniel wasn't happy with. Maybe he didn't want to play them to me.

Flood was doing quite a lot of other stuff and I hadn't seen him in a long time, probably like six months or a year.

Flood, Dave and Fletch came around and had a little look at what we were doing, but mostly Daniel and I were left alone with it. I think the main mixes were done in two weekends and I think we went on and did it and we were all done a week later.

I was brought in specifically to deal with the mix of 'Enjoy The Silence', so I didn't really see Alan, Flood, Fletch and Dave much. I don't think Martin came up. They all eventually loved it though. They said that if it gets officially improved, they would stick with it.

I think in this digital world, we can do things much quicker, but in those days you worked hard to get something to have some sort of flavour or appeal. You hope you get that but you sort of stay inside a project when you're doing it, but now it's almost like you need to get away from it for about 2-3 months and then review it later.

At the playback, I remember Dave hanging off the back of my chair as people often do. For me, there was a bit of a positive vibe there in the studio and again they walked in and what everyone heard was quite pleasing.

There was a bit of nervousness around them because of Dave's well-being. Dave was having some issues and I was just warned about it before they came and asked not to mention anything that seemed off.

I remember seeing the video come out on TV and thinking, "Wow what a great video." I mean it was a *great* video.

I remember we kept the mix very dry, presumably to reflect the demo aspect of it all and I remember thinking, "Wow, this works great when it came across on the TV screen."

When a record blows up you hear it in a different way than when you were making it.

Depeche Mode had talent, they had a vision and they sort of knew what to do – 10 years in the making. They were comfortable in that flow.

Even in those days, machine music was now always 'music'. Sounds laughable now. We were doing something new that nobody had ever done before.

I think 'Violator' has aged fantastically. And, as I always say, the album now appears more relevant now than it did for the year it was created. It does its thing and stays that way. But I think, over time, it's become a more important album than it was at the time.

Daniel and I would chat about how important a record it was for the band. It was huge and we were lucky to be at the right place at the right time. He was very committed to his artists and was probably like the executive producer on most of the records. Especially all the big ones.

David Browne (Ireland), assistant engineer on 'Violator' at Master Rock in London

I was at Master Rock and was one of the assistant engineers at the studios.

I had spent five years working in Dublin as a tape-op and assistant engineer and then moved over to London in 1988. I started working in Jacob Studios in Farnham and then went to Kilburn to work at Master Rock.

I was in my late-20s and was assigned to Depeche. The engineer was Phil (Legg) and then there was Daniel (Miller).

I would have been excited about it but it was just another job. The type of people going to Master Rock then were high-level ones.

I know it sounds blasé but you kind of got used to it, certainly with the type of clients that were in Master Rock.

There were so many different artists coming in – people like Bryan Ferry, who I had worked with on an album called 'Mamouna'.

***

I remember I was going to Los Angeles at the very end of the session. I had packed my suitcase and I brought it around to the studio because I was on an early morning flight to the States, the next day.

I brought my suitcase in and Daniel came into the studio and not the control room, where I put my case.

He said to me, with a very serious face, "David, we are going to need you tomorrow. We are going to be extending the session."

I must have looked shocked because I was going to Los Angeles tomorrow. And he just looked at me, smiled, and said, "Got you!"

So, there was a good atmosphere at the session.

Daniel felt very strongly that he wanted to mix 'Enjoy The Silence' because I think he knew it was going to be such a massive hit for them.

Flood came to visit one day – I only met him briefly – to listen to the mixes that Daniel and Phil had put together.

I showed Flood the recording studio because at Master Rock there was a Focusrite console. There were only ever two of them built. 001 was in Master Rock and 002 was in New York.

One thing I would say about Flood is that he was very down-to-earth.

I remember, bringing him into the control room, starting to explain the desk to him, and he just stopped me halfway and said, "Dave, it doesn't matter. A desk is a desk."

So I realise, "Yeah a desk is a desk, they all do the same thing in slightly different ways."

He wasn't condescending in any way, it was just him putting me at ease and saying, "I know, it is a good desk."

Anyway, the Focusrite console was being used for a different client, so we mixed 'Enjoy The Silence' on an SSL (Solid State Logic) console.

And then it was mixed onto half-inch tape, on a two and a half-inch machine.

I always remember what amazed me about Flood was his memory of each part of the song. Because they played it in the mix and he would come back with a list of suggestions on how to adapt or change the mix.

He would say, "Well, what have you changed here in the first four bars?"

Yet he had no notes written down, it was just in his head.

I remember the band coming in and being asked for my name, just for the credits on the album.

They were incredibly down-to-earth, too. I remember waiting for a taxi in the reception with Dave [Gahan], we were having a conversation and it was just very down-to-earth. No stardom.

I suppose I wasn't a major Depeche Mode fan. I did like the band but I didn't follow a lot of their work.

We were talking about a film ['101'] that had been made in Los Angeles, where they had played to thousands of people.

The session eventually ended with just Daniel, Phil and me, and then I was off to LA the next day.

The final mixes were sent off to the studio for the band to have a listen to.

***

There's definitely a difference in sound between 'Enjoy The Silence' and other songs on the album

They were mixed in different studios, on different consoles, with different approaches – with Daniel mixing Flood's input.

That's probably my opinion in some sense. But I notice that when I play it there is a difference in sound compared to some of the other tracks on the album.

It's hard to describe because when you talk about sound, it's very subjective.

It's really hard to define what one person hears. I just take it on the basis of production, and when mixes are done by different people there is going to be a human factor in there, so the tracks will translate individually.

But I couldn't pinpoint it precisely because that would become a defined opinion. I think it basically comes down to the fact that you might hear a difference in the sound, or you might not.

It's interesting when you listen to 'Enjoy The Silence' by Tori Amos because that version is similar to the original version that the guys had.

I always remember Tori Amos's version as I played it a few times at demonstrations for hi-fi, which I later got into. It's very chilling.

***

I think the feeling was that it was Depeche Mode and they had had hits, and it was going to be another one of those hits.

But I had a feeling that this was going to be an iconic hit. You sometimes just think it's another great track and it's only when it gets off on the street that it becomes what it becomes.

'Enjoy The Silence' was different. I've played the album quite a few times since I finished working in studios – now working in and promoting hi-fi.

I worked for a German company in Japan, Korea, Singapore, Malaysia, Hong Kong, Taiwan and I would often play tracks from the album.

If you wanted electronic music... you would play that!

Roberto Baldi (Italy), engineer on 'Violator' at Logic Studio in Milan

We – Pino (Pischetola) and I – started working at Logic studios and, just three months later, the owner of the studio told us that we have a band coming in tomorrow for around six weeks and that it was a British band.

We saw a lot of movement, people getting the studio ready, so I assumed that it was probably a big band – someone famous.

He didn't tell us the name but I was a big fan of them, so it was shocking. When I saw Martin, I just thought:, "Fuck my life – they're really here."

For Pino it was probably the biggest opportunity of his life so far, to work for a band like Depeche Mode. And they were really great with him.

They were very professional – always started at 11 or so in the morning, and worked very intensely for eight to nine hours. They were really focused.

I had a really good relationship with Alan Wilder. We used to be together almost every day.

Both Flood and François Kevorkian were amazing to work with, and François was always full of stories, especially about Kraftwerk.

Every day when he left the studio, Kraftwerk would check him to make sure he didn't leave with any pieces of tape.

They once got a phone call from Michael Jackson asking to do a version of 'The Robots', but they said no. They said no to MJ!

"We don't like people making covers of our music," they said. Michael Jackson was super famous at the time, having just released 'Thriller', so François thought this was really amazing.

The recording process was more complicated back then because everything was slower. Now we reproduce everything with a computer. This was especially so with samples – and they used a lot of samples!

It was a nightmare because every time you had to stretch a sample you would have to spend hours because they used AKAI machines.

At the time I was a producer, but I only helped Depeche with samplers, to organise the work more than anything, to cut this and that – this was my job.

I remember we recorded footsteps for 'Personal Jesus' using the stairs of the building to make part of the rhythm section of the song.

There was also 'Halo', for example, which starts with a rhythmic breath – that's a sample from a porn movie.

I remember there was an Italian singer, she was also in the studio. She saw the movie on a big screen and said, "What are we doing here?!"

The big work was to find new sounds because Martin used to do the demo with standard sounds.

Generally, they didn't like using the same sound that had been used on a previous album, so they needed to find the right sound for different songs, or find samples and put all the stuff together.

Alan was driving a lot of this. Flood, too, but he was also finding sound effects for songs that were already recorded.

But the creation of the sounds was mostly Alan and Martin.

I remember that the Fletch was doing a lot of the samples. They came with a big box of vinyl and we spent one day listening to everything, to find something to sample. Fletch was really into that.

Flood always used distortive stuff, too, for a more aggressive sound. If you think about earlier Depeche Mode, before 'Violator', they always used to be clean – electronic but really clean.

But Flood was dirtier – he added that dirty element to the band.

***

We used to go out almost every night. All together. We used to always use my car!

They really liked the clubs in Milan, listening to the music, and sitting with the people – they were really kind to everybody, including fans.

We used to have three big clubs. One of the most famous was called Hollywood where we go to relax after work.

Because they always seemed to be very focused on everything, I think they liked to go out for a couple of hours to the clubs, just to meet some people, hear some music, and see the reactions.

Once they also played a song, in a club, to test it. But they were so famous. So every time we used to get to the club, there would be a lot of people outside. "Oh, Depeche Mode!"

I think they were really satisfied with everything but I also remember that on the day they left, I felt really sad. Alan said, "I know how you feel because I feel this way, too, because we spent three months together."

I have worked with a lot of artists in my life, but during the three months for 'Violator', everything was perfect and everyone seemed very happy. Nothing went wrong and there were no problems.

I think they really loved what they did. I am sure about that. I remember Daryl (Bamonte), Daniel, Flood – everyone was really happy.

When they worked on 'Violator', it looked more friendly compared to now. It felt like they were really good friends.

Everybody lives in a different place now, so it's more like a job.

Nils Tuxen (Denmark), pedal steel guitar on 'Clean'

I was working in my native country, Denmark, in the Puk recording studios on a follow-up album with the German group, Moti Special, with fellow group member Dicky Tarrach and our arranger, Werner Becker, for Polydor (now Universal).

We had a couple of hits in the mid-1980s, most notably 'Cold Days, Hot Nights', which reached number three in the German charts, and after some personnel changes in the line-up, we were finishing the recording and were starting to mix it at Puk.

Depeche Mode were working on 'Violator' in the other studio, and I guess the studio manager and engineer Peter Iversen had told the guys about the fact that I play pedal steel guitar, besides guitar.

Anyway, I was asked if I would be willing to come over to their studio to do some recording for them.

I was aware of them, and although not a fan, I did and do appreciate their work.

My contribution all took place at Puk studios, which are located outside of Randers in Denmark.

I had been working there regularly for a number of years and witnessed how the studio grew from a small local recording studio to a huge complex with two fantastic studios, three or four houses with three bedrooms in each, a good chef to cater for the studio clients and an extra building with a huge swimming pool and sauna, as well as sports facilities beside a beautiful park-like garden with an outdoor chess board for recreational purposes.

Puk at that time had become an internationally popular studio with artists like George Michael and Elton John being regular clients. As a studio musician, I had worked there for, among others, Scottish band Danny Wilson, Ray Sawyer of Dr. Hook and LaToya Jackson.

I actually didn't hear anything of what Depeche were working on. And I wasn´t told any titles. As a matter of fact, I didn't know what song the steel guitar was used on until my daughter, Emilie, told me that she had found some information about this on the internet.

The session took place in this way: I brought my steel guitar and an amp over to their studio, and it was hooked up to a DAT recorder. I was asked to record anything that came to my mind on the DAT tape without any other musical signals – no melody, no chords and no timing.

So in a way, it was a very experimental way of making music that I have never tried before nor after.

I was free to play anything I wanted. There was, as I recall it, no instruction whatsoever.

As I recall it, only Alan and the engineer Peter Iversen were present as I was recording. Martin and Dave were around but not in the studio, whereas Andy was in London and as I recall. Flood, too, was absent the day I was working.

When I bought the album and listened to it, I had no idea where my instrument had been used, and I didn't recognize it anywhere on any of the titles on the album. Until years later, when my daughter found the information that it was on the title 'Clean' that Alan had used samples of the steel guitar, but still I don't know where and what parts were used.

I´m still honoured that they asked me.

As I try to do in any recording situation, I tried to give my best. I´m glad and grateful that Alan obviously found something he could use; otherwise, I would not have been credited on the cover, I guess. But the aspect of using samples is still foreign to the way I make music.

Depeche Mode are the biggest name for whom I´ve so far worked as a studio musician.

Paul Kendall (UK), harmonica on 'Personal Jesus' and studio engineer

Since getting my first Dansette [record player] at seven, I had always been interested in music, particularly songs with exotic sounds – 'Telstar' was an early favourite.

At 14, we had our first band, an adolescent blues trio – I was singing and playing recorder and harmonica; Steve played guitar and Ray was our bongo man – we were called Obscenity's Children.

By 17, I was blowing free jazz sax in the local youth club. For me, it was primarily about the sound and not particularly the music.

I went off to the University of York to read Maths but lasted only two terms after spending the majority of time in the music department playing with a VCS3 and a Revox tape recorder and not attending maths lectures.

I briefly considered trying to work in a recording studio but didn't have the connections or knowledge of how to go about it, so ended up working for Barclays Bank in Piccadilly Circus for nine and a half years (I was down for 10 but got out earlier on good behaviour!).

During this time, with two friends, we set up a small rehearsal studio in a Covent Garden basement and people would rehearse their bands or we'd record demos for them. We had no multitrack recording, so we'd record the bass and drums on one tape machine, play it back whilst adding the guitars onto another tape machine, building the mix layer by layer.

This was my sole prior experience of a 'recording' studio!

In 1984 I was fortunate enough to be able to say *au revoir* to Barclays Bank. I'd inherited some money and was able to buy a newly available and affordable 16-track tape recorder and a small mixing console.

My first wife, Joni, was a backing singer with Fad Gadget so I had met Daniel Miller a few times. 'Warm Leatherette' was the only Mute record I owned.

I mentioned to him that I'd just bought the Fostex 16-track and an Allen & Heath desk; he had been considering exactly the same gear for Mute to set up a rehearsal / recording space for the label.

Consequently, he asked me to get involved and soon I was ferrying the monster that was the Synclavier to studios around the world from Adrian Sherwood in Southern to Daniel / Depeche Mode in Hansa in Berlin, Puk in Denmark and Guillaume Tell in Paris.

Eventually, after about 18 months in a temporary studio at the top of Rough Trade in Collier Street, we had two purpose-built rooms in the main Mute office in Harrow Road.

The principal studio was christened Worldwide International and had a small recording space sufficient to record a drum kit and a large control room where most of the work was done. And for the next ten years, I lived most of my life there and in the smaller room, christened The Means Of Production – or programming suite, as it was more commonly known.

Both rooms facilitated not just Mute artists but by now 429 Harrow Road had Rhythm King, Blast First, Product Inc artists too. Betty Boo in the programming suite and the Butthole Surfers in Worldwide - endless joy in the studio kitchen. The Laibach occupation of 1991 took over three rooms, as we had added a digital editing suite on my insistence.

The arrival of Depeche in our world was an important test for the studio. Daniel had suggested they start their 'Violator' pre-production work in the programming suite. Quite possibly these were the first sessions with Flood. No idea.

Flood had spent many long days in Worldwide, already working with Renegade Soundwave and Nitzer Ebb, a man of prodigious talent across the musical spectrum, jaw-droppingly patient and a very nice man from whom I learnt much.

I can't recall exact details about the set-up for Flood with Depeche but it would certainly involve AKAI and Emulator samplers, Roland 100M synth modules and an Arp or two, and definitely a Roland Jazz Chorus 40 amp.

One day I was working next door and Flood came in, and says, "Oi, PK, you play the harmonica, have you got five minutes?" It's not very often you get summoned to perform the harmonica for Flood but he knows how to go straight to a noise man's heart by insisting that we record it through the aforementioned JC40 with a veneer of distortion.

I performed a few percussive in-out breath chugs on the low end of probably a G Hohner Echo Super Vamper, my harp of preference back then. To my absolute joy, my chug is immortalised in 'Personal Jesus' coming in around one minute and is a recognizable part of the rhythm track. Should have retired then!

From those early days of 'Violator' and my five minutes of glory, I had no involvement in the process, although I do remember the studio kitchen being filled to the brim with flight cases of the equipment hired in for François Kervorkian's mixing. I was also responsible for getting the equipment from the UK to Puk and setting it up for the start of the sessions.

It was a great album and Flood had succeeded in creating a new Depeche sound, aided and abetted by Alan [Wilder] and Daniel, with François as the fresh ears.

I did get to dip my toe in the water again when Daniel booked Worldwide for a block of eight days for me to assist and engineer four different remixes of 'Enjoy The Silence', known as the Quad Final Mix.

Now I can remember it not being my favourite track, despite its later success, but I had to listen to the same song for eight days through four different pairs of ears. I was over. I nearly retired then.

On the positive side it was intriguing working with Tim [Simenon], Holger [Hiller], Gareth [Jones] and Adrian Sherwood].

Chris Snoddon (Northern Ireland), fan

Depeche Mode had always intrigued me with their electronics and I found, as I had grown older, that the maturity of their work seemed to grow with me.

I was 17 years old, soon to turn 18, and I found the music to be uplifting in a real-life kind of sense that I, as with many others of a similar generation, felt we could relate to.

My excitement was driven by the single releases prior to 'Violator's arrival, with 'Personal Jesus' being given to me by a friend on 12-inch around October / November 1989, and the monumental 'Enjoy The Silence' blasting what seemed like hourly on the Radio 1 playlist that February.

'Personal Jesus' was a strange release for me, as traditionally I wasn't very keen on guitars, but the blues riff was so infectious that when I was offered the 12-inch I nearly snapped my mate's hand off, as much for the fact that it was a DM record as opposed to me loving the track.

I played it for the first time expecting an extended play of the radio version and couldn't believe what I had just obtained, as the Holier Than Thou Approach remix left the blues stomping and turned instead to hypnotic electro pulsing.

I knew that this band were onto a new level, with production so crisp and clean it nearly shone. What a gem.

The Western brothel-style video also complimented the track with its grainy ambience and busty señoritas, portraying the band as cowboys stopping off at a Texan-style parlour house for some female companionship.

This feeling about the new material was only reinforced when 'Enjoy The Silence' was released. Again, a guitar riff stole the show but the disco drum beat and robotic bassline set this track ahead of anything I had heard before and made my anticipation for what was to come from 'Violator' even greater.

Again, a video was made that, although I thought weird at first, was so arty and leftfield I could only describe it as pure brilliance. In truth, it was only many a year later when I listened to an interview with Martin that I actually understood Anton Corbijn's concept for this.

I got into Belfast city centre after college on release day and made my way to Makin Tracks records on Castle Lane, picking up 'Violator' on cassette from the new release section.

It stood out automatically at the time as a Depeche cover, firstly due to it being black and because I could associate the red rose on the cover as bearing a similar styling to the white rose for the 'Enjoy The Silence' sleeve.

The opening riff of 'World In My Eyes' started as I listened intently and I immediately thought that it didn't grab me as the two singles did. Nothing intrigued me about it, it just ambled along with its sparse spacious synths and didn't have any major chord deviation that sparked excitement in me.

'Sweetest Perfection' then started with the fading in drum roll and what sounded to me at the time like a sampled guitar that progressed through involving a scything metallic noise to the stringed middle eight.

I remember thinking, "This sounds like too many real instruments, not synthesisers. What are they playing at here?!"

'Personal Jesus' gave me a glimmer that things were looking up as I now loved the track, especially as it had the extended electronic elements at the end

And then 'Halo', again introducing heavy 'real' orchestral sounds that just threw me again. Even though the previous albums weren't all a bundle of laughs this one was definitely bringing serious to a new level.

'Waiting For The Night', although fascinating in parts, didn't instantly strike me like previous downtempo tracks, as I couldn't relate to it and it seemed too mature for me.

'Enjoy The Silence' was electronic perfection but my understanding of the drawn-out, high-pitched note ebbing away to the sinister 'Crucified' was non-existent, featuring a further guitar riff and a voice sample akin to something from a 'Hellraiser' movie. I just didn't see the point of it at that time.

'Policy Of Truth' started as a disappointment, as a clear guitar sample was being used as the lead line and the saxophone-style sound being introduced after the chorus made me shudder.

This alone was enough to put me off the song, as I was so inclined to detest anything 'normal' and 'real' instrumentation-wise at the time that I couldn't see the actual brilliance within the layering of the track.

'Blue Dress' and 'Clean' both appeared meandering as well, and I had a distaste for the Ennio Morricone, soundtrack-style breeze through 'Clean' as it didn't sound synthetic enough for my liking. I also couldn't fathom at the time the need to add the eerie scratching sounds between the two tracks at the beginning and end of the musical infill 'Interlude'.

Admittedly, 'Violator' deflated me after the first listen and I tried to revisit it on a number of occasions in the ensuing days but I found it a struggle to get past 'Enjoy The Silence'.

The reason I didn't think it was on a par with the previous albums was that it sounded so mature in my eyes, with a soundscape that was almost filmic and not suited to an electronic band who should only be using synths.

This mood lasted for me for around six months, where I continued to try and like it but I was finding it hard making the album tracks work for me as I was still on a daily diet of Erasure, Pet Shop Boys and early 1980s electronic which included most of Depeche Mode up to 'Music For The Masses' and '101'.

'World In My Eyes' had started to grow on me, as it always got a listen being the first track. When it was released as a single, I bought the 12-inch and now, I had the 'Personal Jesus' and 'Enjoy The Silence' vinyl and added 'Policy Of Truth' as well to complete the 'Violator' collection.

The Beat Box remix of 'Policy Of Truth' was the turning point for me, as throughout the mix I could easily hear how the layers of the track had been structured and sonically developed to turn what I thought was a mediocre track into a piece of real innovation and class.

I started to play 'Violator' through my Sennheiser headphones, attempting to try and locate every little sound that had been used to construct the final tracks and it was then that I finally got the album. To this day I look at 'Violator' as a whole entity, from start to finish, not as a collection of nine different songs.

Looking at the team involved with 'Violator', I can now see why their contribution saw this album turn out so brilliantly. All masters in their respective fields, with a wealth of knowledge from working with some of the most respected artists in the business such as Kraftwerk and U2.

Although Flood has worked with Depeche since Violator on 'Songs Of Faith And Devotion', and as recently as 'Delta Machine', one can't help but wonder what a further album with all those respective players in place (François Kevorkian, Flood and Depeche Mode with Alan) would have been like and if it would have made further sonic progression.

The soundscape of 'Violator' definitely propelled Depeche onto a new level and the structuring and depth of the next album, 'Songs Of Faith And Devotion', can be associated with 'Violator' as it again progresses through in a cinematic depth, albeit in a more raw, industrial styling.

Changes to the band saw a change in style from the heavily layered atmospheric soundscapes, but the influence that 'Violator' had on other groups was immense and helped change the synth landscape for many.

Erasure for one appeared to turn tail and go the opposite direction to how real and mature 'Violator' seemed, dropping the subtle electronics used through 'The Innocents' and 'Wild!' in the late 1980s for a very obvious analogue synthetic style on 'Chorus' which they have continued using to this day.

The Pet Shop Boys also adopted a slightly more mature sound when they released 'Behaviour' later in 1990, compared to 1988's overtly electronic 'Introspective'.

The tracks on 'Violator' that I didn't find interesting or exciting on the first hearing now hypnotise me with the detail used in their construction, with 'Sweetest Perfection' now moving me so much that it is one of the stars of the album.

This was only reinforced when I first played the 5.1 Surround Audio version from the remasters in 2006 and, again, it brought with it a sonic element that I had never before experienced from the stereo version.

In fact, every track from the remaster package brought some new element from the respective tracks to the fore and to this day it is the medium I prefer to play when I revisit 'Violator'.

I now find it very hard to say there is a weak track on the album. The attention to detail throughout all the tracks is something that I don't believe I have heard on an album since.

Logic Studio team, Milan, May 1989 - L to R: Andy Fletcher, Alan Wilder, Daryl Bamonte, Roberto Baldi (engineer), Martin Gore, David Gahan, Flood (producer)... (Credit: Roberto Baldi)

Milan, May 1989 - L to R: Andy Fletcher, Dave Gahan, Pino Pischetola (engineer), Flood (producer), Alan Wilder, Martin Gore, Daryl Bamonte… (Credit: Roberto Baldi)

Puk studio complex, Randers, Denmark… (Credit: Peter Iversen)

Depeche Mode performing 'Personal Jesus' on Peter's Pop Show, Germany, November 1989… (Credit: unknown)

'Personal Jesus', 'Enjoy The Silence', 'Policy Of Truth', 'World In My Eyes' singles… (Credit: David McElroy)

Violator album signing event, Wherehouse Records, Los Angeles, March 1990… (Credit: Mike LaJoie)

David Gahan filming a mimed performance of 'Enjoy The Silence' for French TV, South Tower, World Trade Center, New York City, March 1990… (Credit: Michael Lyons)

'Violator' LP designs, top: Venezuela, Mexico, Brazil… lower: Benelux, Sweden, Spain… (Credit: David McElroy)

Poster for Dodger Stadium show, with Electronic and Nitzer Ebb supporting, Los Angeles, Summer 1990… (Credit: unknown)

Logic Studio, Milan, May 1989 - Andy Fletcher and Martin Gore...
(Credit: Roberto Baldi)

Andy Fletcher between takes for a mimed performance of 'Enjoy The Silence' for French TV, South Tower, World Trade Center, New York City, March 1990… (Credit: Michael Lyons)

'Violator' UK releases, clockwise: Vinyl LP, CD, Minidisc, Cassette, DCC… (Credit: David McElroy)

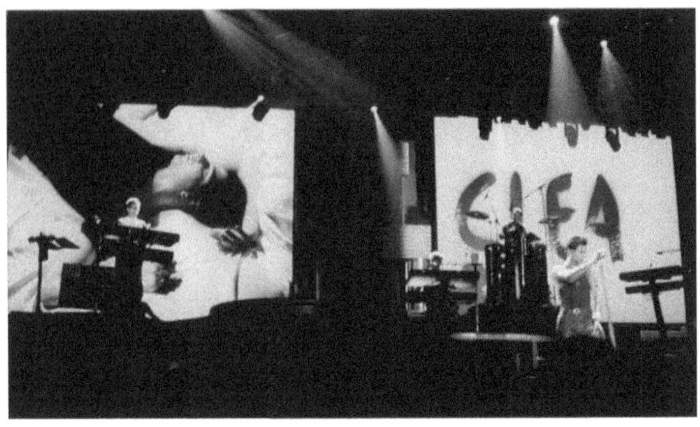

Depeche Mode performing at Wembley Arena on the World Violation Tour, November 1990… (Credit: Michael Rose)

Depeche Mode performing at Wembley Arena on the World Violation Tour, November 1990… (Credit: Kevin May)

Commemorative double platinum disc for 2 million sales of 'Violator', given to engineer Steve Lyon… (Credit: Kevin May)

Dave Gahan and studio engineer Roberto Baldi, reunited in New York City, 2018… (Credit: Roberto Baldi)

Lyrics to 'Halo' on a London Underground information board, Tufnell Park station, 2018… (Credit: Sean Kelly)

Chapter 4

Cowboys, A King And A Rose

"Every video we've ever done with Anton... has been fun. Every photo session that we've ever done with Anton... is fun. Take Anton out of the equation... it's a nightmare."

***

By the late-1980s, Depeche Mode had largely managed to rid the pop moniker that had been hanging around their necks since they had bounced playfully onto the scene with their debut album, 'Speak & Spell' in 1981.

Yet this had not been an easy task.

The change in the perception of the music by fans and a growing number of critics had actually come about relatively early, not least with the release of singles such as 'Blasphemous Rumours' in 1984.

On its release, the song perfectly illustrated the growing feeling that Martin Gore had a lot more depth to his craft than a unique ability to pen a catchy pop tune, such as Everything Counts from the previous album.

The outwardly shy chief songwriter was clearly able to explore and vocalise difficult issues such as suicide and loss.

Again, 'Master And Servant' may have been an upbeat slice of classic, mid-1980s electronica, but the lyrics turned to a subject matter (BDSM) that was not one normally associated with a band that until then had appeared on more than their fair share of teeny-bop TV shows and teenage magazine front covers.

The 'Black Celebration' album, arriving in 1986, had pushed the growing awareness of Depeche's musical scope and intensity even further.

Yet for all the maturity and complexity that was emerging within the songwriting, coupled with accessible but obvious darkness creeping into the arrangements and production of the songs, visually the boys still had a tremendously steep mountain to climb.

Many of their television appearances are now often rather painful to watch; indeed, their fresh-faced, pin-up faces that adorned magazines around Europe failed to shine much of a light at all on the concentrated effort behind the scenes to add layers of complexity to their music.

The videos in particular were generally a mixture of somewhat giddy, sugar-coated pieces to camera, especially from frontman Dave Gahan, or simply four-minute slabs of a concept or theme of sorts that had no overall connection to either the song or the general mood surrounding a particular musical period.

Two low points from their promotional appearances on television and the early videos will immediately come to the minds of many fans: awkwardly (and bizarrely) cradling chickens as they perform 1982 hit single 'See You' in a mocked-up farmyard in a TV studio on German television show Bananas, and the video for 'It's Called A Heart' in 1985.

It is somewhat inconceivable now that Depeche would have even agreed to participate in something so peculiar as the scene set for the performance of 'See You', or rush through head-high reeds of grass for the video accompanying 'It's Called A Heart'- looking very much like countless other Brits who had just stepped off a plane from a Mediterranean holiday, with glowing facial tans - as they belt out the weakest single the band had recorded in years.

Pop videos accompanying pop songs had an unwritten requirement to perhaps portray the artist like, well, pop stars.

These somewhat lightweight activities obviously brought Depeche to a wide audience of pop-loving teenagers, often indicated in part by the demographic, and associated screaming, of those who attended their gigs.

For a long time, such a strategy was in fact a rather successful one, created to support an image that couldn't be broken.

But as the music hardened around the time of 'Some Great Reward', Depeche's visual output began to sit increasingly awkwardly in contrast to what the fans were hearing, or interpreting.

'Master And Servant', the second single from the 'Some Great Reward' album in 1984, is an obvious example of this odd juxtaposition between the edgier audio and flimsy, if rather odd, video representation.

Gahan jumps around a lot, as he was often seen doing in many of the band's previous videos. Gore, Wilder and Andy Fletcher mime some backing vocals. Fletch is seen earnestly using a jackhammer. Someone rolls around on the floor, hands bound by chains.

And all this is interspersed with footage from Greenham Common (the infamous military base in the UK where American cruise missiles were based), the United Nations and suburban new-build homes. The video, directed by Clive Richardson, is peculiar, to say the least.

Fans will no doubt point to other examples in the group's visual record up to that point in the mid-1980s, such as 'Get The Balance Right' and 'People Are People', where the emerging quality of the songs was not matched by how the band was portrayed when in the hands of video directors or TV producers. Famously, Kevin Hewitt, who directed the video for 'Get The Balance Right', knew so little about the band that he thought Alan was, in fact, the lead singer.

Yet the aforementioned video for 'It's Called A Heart', created by Peter Care, may have been a turning point of sorts.

Musically it was a strikingly upbeat ode to heartache which acted as a handy book-end - especially when coupled with the equally bubbly debut single 'Dreaming Of Me' from 1981 – to a period in Depeche's history, something that clearly wasn't lost on the marketers at Mute who used the track as the radio play fodder for the 'Singles 81-85' collection which was released in October 1985.

But it also marked the end of an era in Depeche's visual history.

From then on, despite using Care and Richardson respectively to direct the videos for the 'Stripped' and 'A Question of Lust' singles from 'Black Celebration' in 1986, Depeche's music just simply couldn't be supported by the look and feel of any of the band's previous visual outings.

(Most fans know the story behind 'But Not Tonight', an up-tempo track which was originally slated to be the B-side to 'Stripped'. The band's US label, Sire, chose the song as the lead track on the single due to its inclusion on the soundtrack for the woeful 'Modern Girls' movie, starring Virginia Madsen and Cynthia Gibb. It was directed by Tamra Davis and shot specifically to include cut-aways from the movie.)

The apparent and deliberate bleakness and depth of 'Black Celebration' coincided with an obvious maturing in the band's overall image.

Darker clothes, noticeably fewer photo shoots with the band grinning like pop stars, and an alternative edge to their look fuelled the idea within and outside the Depeche camp that, after six years, they deserved to be taken more seriously than before.

***

At the time there were arguably very few photographers in the business like Anton Corbijn, the lanky Dutchman who had carved out a name for himself as an up-and-coming snapper on the 'New Musical Express' weekly newspaper in the UK.

Corbijn had an uncanny ability to transform even the most unlikely musical artists into fashionable icons, but often not in a conventional way. During 'Inside Out', a 2012 film-length biopic of Corbijn, James Hetfield, frontman of Metallica, said "he can make anyone look cool."

His catalogue of photography is, nowadays, a remarkable who's-who of the music world over the course of the last 35 years, with some of the most iconic pictures ever taken of many groups coming via his lens, in particular, Joy Division, U2 and David Bowie.

Still, in the mid-1980s Corbijn was mostly known for his still camerawork, rather than the moving image, having directed just a handful of music videos.

He had of course already taken photographs of Depeche in their very early days at Blackwing Studio for the 'NME' when Vince Clarke was still a member of the group. Dave hated the photo that the 'NME' used for their cover shot as he was blurred and out of focus with the other three band members presented normally. Corbijn didn't enjoy working with the band at that time, deeming them "too poppy."

Perhaps mirroring the newfound confidence and edge of their recorded work, Depeche Mode handed Corbijn the task of directing the video for 'A Question of Time', the last single from 'Black Celebration'.

Shot over a scorching few days in California in July 1986, Corbijn later confessed that he only took the job because he wanted to work in the US where Depeche just happened to be at the time, three-quarters of the way through the 'Black Celebration Tour'.

The video, shot in Corbijn's trademark black and white, was a far simpler affair from a production point of view than previous efforts, using a mixture of live footage from the band's Irvine Meadows gigs and some staged work at a house in Los Angeles.

Wilder later said, "He was easy to work with; he had one camera, a producer and maybe one other person doing a bit of lighting – and that was all there was to it, and we really liked that.

"We'd been used to up until that point of working with big film crews; disinterested sparks in the background taking the piss while you're trying to do something that's not natural to you anyway. We hated the whole set-up.

"So when this person came along it was fresh, it was easy, he had a good sense of humour."

The die was cast, with Gahan – as the band's frontman – inevitably on the lion's share of the visual focus. Gahan, a former-art college student before going full-time with Depeche Mode, especially liked Corbijn's relaxed, unconventional methods and quirky creative style.

Gahan now says that Corbijn had become an "integral part of the development of Depeche Mode, visually.

"We work hand in hand and he enhances what we do music-wise with his visuals. That can be a photograph, that can be a film that we use onstage to enhance a particular song or a moment in a particular performance.

"I think Anton understands our music, and I think for a while we were lost in the early days looking for something that was visual to latch on to. Anton really was the key that unlocked that door for us."

Talking to 'The Independent' in 2011, Corbijn is equally flattering about Gahan."He's so great-looking it's hard to be photographed with him; you look like a loser. He is a great performer, and I realised he has acting potential; he was naturally quite good at interpreting things."

Unlocking the confidence, humour and some slithers of a genuine talent for acting in frontman Gahan was only part of the equation as to why Corbijn and the band had managed to forge the start of a solid and creative relationship.

Another was Corbijn's ability to come up with ideas that challenged the proforma of what a music video should be, especially for Depeche Mode.

In the hands of another director, 'A Question Of Time' might have had the four members of Depeche Mode running about in a watchmaker's store, or some other cringe-worthy, literal interpretation of the song's lyrics.

Instead, Corbijn cut live footage of the band performing onstage during the 'Black Celebration Tour' in the US with a sequence where Alan Wilder, who agreed to do some extra filming in between gigs, waits impatiently for the delivery of a baby from an unkempt motorcycle courier.

Wilder is then joined by his three band-mates who mess around with some other babies (there are a few clocks here and there, admittedly) while the rider is seen crashing his bike in the desert.

The final outcome, in some respects, doesn't make a whole lot of sense, and yet it's a great video – the live shows look lively and intense, and there's a completely different aesthetic to the band that is unseen in previous videos, not least with the closing bars of the song even momentarily capturing them looking relaxed, natural and laughing as a baby pulls on Gore's wiry hair.

The quirkiness and upbeat look and feel of 'A Question of Time' gave way to a far seedier affair when Corbijn was asked to make the video for 'Strangelove', the first single from 'Music For The Masses'.

The video was shot in Paris, where the band recorded the vast majority of the album at Guillaume Tell Studios, and featured various women writhing around in a darkened Parisian apartment with very little clothing on, while the band looked moody and – for the first time in their video output – rather cool as they posed on the streets of the French capital in black leather.

This creative departure for the band was helped by another element that was central to Anton Corbijn's aesthetic at the time – his almost unswerving commitment to the use of the Super 8 film format.

The grainy, hand-held style was his signature template for videos, similar to the cross-processing film developing technique that was used in his photography.

Combined with Corbijn's often off-kilter imagination, Depeche Mode now had an identity that they'd never before possessed at all – cool, fairly mysterious, arty, serious.

Perhaps somewhat strangely, Depeche had never struggled with the artwork for their recorded material in the same way that they had in other areas of their image.

Most of their album or single sleeves, apart from the band member-focused 'The Singles 81-85' collection in 1985, had a strong identity and often used striking iconography or edgy subject matter.

The most recent studio long-player before 1990, 'Music For The Masses', was the band's most coordinated and accomplished effort so far in trying to create an identity throughout an era of work, yet it still was arguably not at the level of a single art director attempting to instil a visual framework for how the band wanted to be perceived.

The seeds for what would eventually become over thirty years of collaboration began with the cover artwork for the '101' movie and album cover, both of which featured Corbijn's distinctive images from the show in Pasadena and elsewhere on the tour in North America.

A decision was then made to effectively hand over the reins for all Depeche's artwork and video output for the next project to Corbijn, including videos and artwork for four singles, album sleeve, tour backdrop videos, merchandise and pretty much everything else that is associated with official material.

It was, in modern parlance, a complete branding exercise across multiple products in various formats.

This was a significant undertaking for the Dutchman, who until that point in his career had created videos and photographs that were used on record sleeves, but had not assumed a role that in any other type of organisation would be known as a chief creative officer.

Corbijn had a team with some key people in it to help him: Richard Bell, who had produced a few of his earlier videos for Depeche Mode, alongside Richard Smith at the Area design agency.

The trio, under Corbijn's leadership and often working from basic ideas and sketches, set about formulating a series of projects under the 'Violator' umbrella, most notably the sleeve artwork and videos.

Even though the entire project was coordinated centrally, there was no overall theme attached, other than on the similar combination of a flower and title typeface for the 'Enjoy The Silence' single and the album itself.

There was also nothing to specifically connect the sleeve artwork to the videos for the singles, other than the extremely short use of a flashing rose in the video for 'Enjoy The Silence'.

Branding specialists would no doubt recoil at the lack of coordination but it worked, demonstrating that although the ideas were coming from one person and his team, there was enough creativity to develop visual identities for each micro-project within the 'Violator' canon of work.

What made Corbijn's work so interesting and impressive during this period is that there is arguably no outright, standalone piece. The 'Violator' sleeve, leaning toward irony, like the title itself, with a delicate red rose on a black background, obviously embodied the era but each of the other singles are immersive and striking for other reasons.

'Personal Jesus' has simplicity, led by the subtle use of a cross and the obligatory black and white photo on the rear; 'Enjoy

The Silence's blue background is brighter and the lighter side of the connection to the 'Violator' rose; 'Policy Of Truth' is classic cross-processed photography of a model, and 'World In My Eyes' features a silhouette of each band member creating eyes with their fingers.

Such is the strength of the work that some elements are still felt today in the modern Depeche Mode experience, as fans recreate the eye outlines with their fingers at gigs whenever 'World In My Eyes' is played.

Interestingly, although Corbijn and Smith's work on the sleeves is remarkable, memorable and iconic, many will argue that it was his work with the videos that ensured the 'Violator' era is remembered for more than just a classic album of music.

The freedom that he was given to push forward his ideas for how each song would be represented in the moving image was a symbol of how far and how quickly the relationship between the artist and the band had developed.

Each video, again, had its own identity, such as the seedy bordello in Wild West America (actually filmed in Spain), with local models being recruited to act as members of the establishment.

There was also a grainy, rainy New York City featured in the outdoor scenes for the 'Policy Of Truth' video. A drive-in movie theatre and miniature toy car were used for 'World In My Eyes' alongside footage from a gig on the 'World Violation Tour' earlier that summer.

It is the video for 'Enjoy The Silence' that remains the most memorable, with Gore, Fletch and Wilder having barely noticeable roles compared to that taken on by Gahan.

The video was conceived as a way of portraying someone important who has everything, but who is ultimately looking for some peace and quiet.

Corbijn, Bell and a small crew including band assistant Daryl Bamonte and tour manager Andy Franks, took Gahan on a whirlwind tour of three Europe locations to film him trudging through the snowy Alps, up hills in Scotland and onto beaches in Portugal.

But rather than in his usual garb of black leather, Gahan was dressed as a king to symbolise the notion of someone who has everything and carried a deckchair the entire time.

Gahan, director Corbijn, Bell and many others associated with the band have joked about the absurdity of the video over the years, especially the idea of making the charismatic frontman face march across physically demanding landscapes, miming the song and trying to look relaxed in his chair.

Yet all recognise how important a moment it was in the history of Depeche Mode, with the director and his protegé Gahan illustrating that bizarre ideas can also be done in an incredibly cool and unique way – but by a band who many did not consider cool at all.

***

The collaboration between Corbijn and the band has continued for decades since but, arguably, apart from 'In Your Room' and 'Walking In My Shoes' videos from the 'Songs Of Faith And Devotion' era (and perhaps the 'Suffer Well' single from

2005), such a peak combination of creativity and timing has not been achieved since.

The 'Violator' period work by Corbijn continued through the tour video backdrops, again utilising some of the artwork from the associated video output but with some playful elements, such as Gore dressed as an angel during 'Waiting For The Night' and all band members messing about during 'Personal Jesus'.

Furthermore, the four videos from the singles were included in the mini collection of work from the director, called 'Strange Too', which was released ahead of the final few shows on the tour in November 1990.

More footage from the drive-in video shoot was used, alongside original videos for unreleased tracks from the album, 'Halo' and 'Clean'.

The first featured all members of the band, plus two dancers, filmed at a hillside location in Los Angeles, where Gahan (as the circus strongman) and Gore (as a clown) played out a love triangle with a female circus performer. Fletcher and Wilder, inevitably but probably ironically, were undertakers carrying signs with some of the iconography and typeface from the era.

Again, it's a classic Corbijn and Depeche Mode combination, with the director himself even making a cameo appearance.

'Clean' was a far simpler affair, with Gore the only member present in a sexually-charged sequence of him and a companion (Angela Shelton) watching clips of video material from the band, before engaging in some fairly intense kissing on the couch. There wasn't much to it but it still had an impact.

The video was filmed in Corbijn and Bell's rented apartment in Los Angeles.

What is perhaps remarkable about these two videos is they also speak to the work ethic that the band had once they were on the road.

They were filmed during a week-long stretch that also included three gigs in San Diego, one in Universal City and the two landmark shows at the Dodger Stadium in Los Angeles.

The artwork and video output during the 'Violator' era was not the first work created by the band and their close friend Corbijn, and it was not the last - but, stage and video design for the 'Devotional Tour' in 1993 aside, it arguably stands as the best that they produced together.

The master craftsman and his apprentices were, by this point, in full creative flow and, although they would never admit it, probably couldn't live with the quirky Dutchman pulling the strings.

Richard Bell (New Zealand), video producer for the 'Violator' singles and tour backdrops

The first thing I was involved in with Depeche Mode was ‘A Question of Time’.

I was a system producer at Vivid, a production company, at the time. Anton Corbijn got ‘A Question of Time’ and I got lucky – I was getting a promotion and people were thinking I could do it, so I helped set that up.

We then filmed ‘Strangelove’ in Paris. You’re a little, young producer and you go out to make this video with a band you really love.

I got on well with Anton, so he took me out to dinner the night before the shoot and we had oysters and I was violently sick for 24 hours.

I had definitely been a fan of the band. My interest in music combined with my interest in film left me to pursue a music video angle when I left college.

You are involved with the music industry and you get to do your filmmaking stuff, so I had pursued a music video career because of a band like Depeche. They weren’t the only band that I liked but they are a band that you would really like getting on.

Certainly, for me, it was an amazing period of my life because there was lots of positivity and everything associated with that particular project.

We had done some videos for ‘Music For The Masses’ and Anton at the time was still working in black and white on Super 8, exclusively. That is what he filmed on.

We had done enough work with the band by then to create a good relationship with them and with Daniel Miller. It felt good.

But with every new album, the temptation is always, "We have the new album, let's move on and go work with someone else."

But they didn't. They were really happy with how it was going and they said that they would like us to do the first video of the album.

That was a statement, in a way, and really reassuring for Anton. He said that we are going to move from black and white Super 8 to do colour Super 8.

That's a good space to be working in if somebody does suddenly commit. "We really like you and like what you are doing and like your aesthetic, let's make it an even longer turn."

My impression was it all just felt really good.

You have got this photographer who takes amazing photographs and now makes amazing videos.

And then you reach that point where you trust him and he is now a part of the family. He doesn't make the music but he is integral now to the whole thing.

It works and he fits and his sensibility fits and all that sort of thing. I think they felt incredibly comfortable.

Let's be honest, some bands and artists fully realised, back then, the power of videos.

They understood the medium and what it could and couldn't do and how to utilise it to the maximum.

To their credit, the band had really worked that out. And they realised the video was a really great tool for them.

It also didn't need to be something that is a pain or doesn't quite reflect them.

I think they realised, "Wow, we can make films with Anton that completely and utterly encapsulate what we want to have encapsulated. Our fans are enjoying them and loving them and it's growing our fan base."

This period was getting into the golden period of MTV. Nowadays, videos come out on YouTube and, if you're lucky, you can get a bit of a buzz from them.

You don't have a middle ground anymore. But MTV being the only channel and distribution form really for music videos was a gatekeeper then.

And if you could get through the gate, if you worked out a way to get your videos on MTV, it was really exciting. You could get more stuff on MTV and it really did make a difference.

There was probably a correlation between rotation and the number of albums you sold. Suddenly it was a great deal because MTV was doing what it was meant to do.

Over in the States, it made a huge difference.

***

The band came to Anton and said "Right, what are we going to do for this song, 'Personal Jesus'?"

He has a great way of working – he listens to songs lots of times and comes up with his ideas. By then he was definitely considered a confidant of the band.

It was in Spain – a village down in Almeria where Sergio Leone shot all the Spaghetti Westerns.

They had such a little place where you couldn't do much without everybody knowing what you were doing.

If you are going to shoot in there, at those locations, or if you needed a cast, you would have to go to such and such to do it. Otherwise, they would make sure that it didn't happen!

So the girls were all cast locally. But the day of the shoot came and one of them was not a girl we had chosen.

So we looked at her photographs and Anton was like, "What happened? Hang on we asked for girl X and we got girl Z. I don't understand!"

It turned out the local casting agent had decided that we had made a terrible mistake and so he said we should take one girl over another girl that we had chosen.

We took a bathroom in one of the saloons and used that as our makeup and wardrobe area.

Dave would be in more shots than anybody else, obviously.

But generally, Anton would know what he wanted, we would have a plan and we would just work our way through it.

But it was a lot of fun.

Fletch was told that he'd have to ride a horse. Except there wasn't a horse planned at all for him – he'd been totally wound up.

***

Before 'Enjoy The Silence' we had quite a big meeting – it was in the diary and everyone was going to be there. Everyone knew it was an important song.

They said, "What are we going to do, Anton?" and he said, "Oh, a king in a deck chair."

"Great!" And that was the end of the meeting.

I remember thinking, hang on, this was going to be a big meeting and he just went, "King in a deck chair."

It was strange!

And then he has to go write the script but Anton, well, he doesn't exactly write massive scripts anyway and off we went and did the king in the deck chair.

But we reached that point where they trusted Anton and there was thought of him becoming an extra member of the band.

It was a really cool video to do but you have got to have a big buy-in from the band and especially Dave's willingness to do it.

We went miles making that video – in Switzerland for the snow, in Portugal for the beach, a lot of travelling, a lot of driving.

Nothing is simple or straightforward but Dave would do it. I don't remember it being like, "Oh man, we've got to walk up this snowy hill again".

Walking in snow that deep, dragging a deck chair. I remember the weather in Scotland wasn't great but we really battled that. No complaints.

We had a day's filming in Scotland, but it was a day up and a day down. So three days just for Scotland.

The weather there was absolutely terrible – awful! That is a filmmaker's nightmare, where you have got a landscape project and you are going up there and you always believe you are going to get nice weather, and occasionally you don't.

I seem to remember that it probably stopped raining for just 20 minutes, so those were the 20 minutes that we got for the best shot. The whole time it just rained. It was tough, that one.

Then, I went to Switzerland and found the glacier and sorted that out, showed Anton on the videophone and he was happy with it.

So then we all went to Switzerland and did that. That was another day because we had to use the helicopter to get around the snow for the variation of shots.

We then went back to England and then down to Portugal. Anton knew exactly what he wanted in Portugal – I think he had seen something and knew it immediately.

So then it was a question of adding in the other bits from Portugal, so I think we were at least two or three days in Portugal because of all the travelling.

The other segments, with the full band, were filmed in Anton's studio in the UK.

Technically, Super 8 is about the worst possible film format you can work with.

A tiny speck of dust on the lens on 35mm is tiny – it's a pebble on the beach. On Super 8, it's the size of a bus!

We have had so many horrors with our Super 8 stuff over the years. Different problems, misprocessing, this and that. It's a hell of a medium to work with.

***

'Policy Of Truth' was made near the Meatpacking area in Manhattan, in a studio for part of it and then we did stuff around the city. But I remember the lighting was quite tricky.

Anton likes using natural light to a large degree. So you are not doing a huge amount in terms of lighting for 'Enjoy The Silence', for example.

We had a little bit of light on 'Personal Jesus' but not much.

'Policy Of Truth' definitely took a bit of time. That's the thing about Anton's stuff. It's his aesthetic.

The amount of effort he has put into the background, in getting that to happen in that way is actually massive, but it looks so simple.

There's an enormous amount of thought and effort buried inside there, but it's not as apparent because it hasn't got that big flashiness to it.

Super 8 isn't a slick format. It's got a huge grain and is a non-professional format. It was designed for home use.

So, they are not slick videos, generally.

If you had shot 'Enjoy The Silence' on a 35mm film, it would be completely different.

And, I think that's reflected in the music. The sound is right with Depeche.

To me, that would be one of Anton's absolute strengths, photographically and as a filmmaker.

It's the feel of it. If you are looking for parallels between the music and the production on the music side and the filmmaking, those videos and Anton's sense of feel is really good.

The feel is the number one thing. But isn't that true of Depeche as a band? When you go into a Depeche Mode concert and you hear that stuff live, you come away feeling bloody awesome because it feels great.

***

By the point where we did 'World In My Eyes', the band was on tour.

You've always got this thing in music videos – I joke that music video is the bastard child of the music industry and the film industry, in that they were never really meant to meet.

Film crews like to be on set at 7 in the morning, ready to shoot at 7.30, while musicians generally are just going to bed at 9 in the morning!

So by then, there wasn't really much choice. This is what you've got to do because you can't spend time with the band. The tour was pretty full-on and you had to go about it this way.

We shot two gigs and travelled with them. I remember Nitzer Ebb were on tour with them and I was into skateboarding and so were the Nitzer Ebb boys. On some downtime, we went off and went skateboarding together.

With one camera you're not going to get a lot, and so one night Anton would go from one side and one night to the other. It would have been very risky to have gotten it all in one night.

We were never asked to do a live film. Those are two quite different things in terms of production.

Us rolling into Texas with some great cameras and Anton filming – that's it, it was just him and I.

Whereas, in a full live shoot, you've got all the sound recording and venues.

In America, especially, venues are a nightmare because it costs more if you're going to be filmed – the unions have tied it up, I'm sure.

You then have the hassle of losing seats because you need a crane, you want to put cameras here or there.

So the differences are huge – a substantial chunk of money and a substantial chunk of pain.

I've done live films with Depeche ('Devotional' and 'One Night In Paris') and I've done live films with other acts – they are super complicated in terms of sheer production.

You think you're all ready to go and then the venue says, "Oh no, you can't do it here," or, "We want $50,000," and you ask why and they say the union crew is now working on a film, so they need to get this amount of money.

So it can be very complicated doing a live shoot!

***

For 'Halo', used on the 'Strange Too' collection, we were in California, so we're outside and we're shooting with the stronger sunlight, so it doesn't look as grainy.

We had Dave there for a fair bit of time. The others arrived later for a shorter period of time, did their bits and then Martin stayed on and did his bit.

I'm sure Fletch would say that we spend hours and hours with them hanging around!

We always used to try to make sure they had a good time on the set. We didn't drag them there and keep them all day unless we really had a need to do that.

We asked for some dancing girls, but it's not like the shoot we had in Spain for 'Personal Jesus', where the local casting agency is going to swap girls around because the boss thinks we made a bad decision.

You get a lot of girls who can all dance and who are all great characters and so that is always fun.

It was a really fun shoot.

***

The video for 'Clean' was a lot of fun for Martin!

I like that video because that was our front room at the house that we had rented in LA.

We had taken over this house and we all had bedrooms there and we had our editor there who was cutting stuff, so we all hung out there all the time.

We had X amount of money, and we still needed two more videos – so we did the budget and suddenly realised we had very little money and we're still a video short.

So I got this idea that we could do it in the house.

We squeezed a projector in – but there was an issue with getting the projector to work – and everyone is sitting on everybody else's head, almost.

Martin is trying to do his thing with the girl, and everyone has got their backs pressed against the wall because we were using every inch of space possible in the house.

We didn't have to persuade Martin very much to do it.

Let's be honest, you're going to get some bad gigs and some good gigs – and that would go down in the good gigs category!

I think we cast the girl. I don't remember it coming from a romantic connection to anybody.

The incidentals for 'Strange Too' were in Salt Lake City and it was a nightmare, trying to tie in a location where we could get a drive-in where the band also would be on the tour.

It was relatively easy to shoot though.

In the shots where Dave is playing with the toy car, we ended up doing those in the studio. We needed a bit more space for that and that model was quite complex.

Getting the model car right – we had to give them a photograph of the car from the drive-in and then they got the model to match.

I think Anton liked the idea of putting the videos together. It certainly worked with 'Strange' and so it was like we could go a bit further.

It kind of wrapped everything up but it felt right, the idea of going to a drive-in.

Drive-ins were slightly going out of fashion but still pretty cool if you could get a good one.

***

Certainly, for me, it was an amazing period of my life because there was lots of positivity and everything associated with that project.

But that particular album was a big step up for Anton, directorially.

They were also all really good people.

There are lots of bands that I've worked with when I was coming up through the ranks.

When you're making a cup of tea or sweeping the floor and you meet them and you think, "God, you're a real cock you are, you don't deserve this success."

But I never got that sensation with Depeche, they were a good bunch of people.

By the end of 'Strange Too' we got the Grammy nomination for the video – it had sold really well and I thought that I could actually do this job!

I think I was one of the youngest music video producers in London when I started, fresh out of university.

But I got some lucky breaks, and ended up starting a company and working with Anton and Depeche Mode.

Richard Smith (USA), art designer at Area

My first job out of school was working for a guy called Peter Saville, who was famous for doing Joy Division and New Order.

In the late 1980s, Anton came to Peter Saville to do his book, 'Famouz Photographs 1975-1988', his first, and somehow that landed on my plate to do.

It was a labour of love for him and for me. I obviously had sort of admired all of his photos for years. so he and I sort of struck up a relationship and I basically helped him put that book together.

In 1989, my then-wife Cara and I decided to leave Peter Saville and set up our own business, Area.

We were out with Anton just after his book had been published, celebrating, and he said he was working on the new Depeche Mode single, 'Personal Jesus'.

I said to him, "Well, let me know if you need any help with putting the stuff together," and so sure enough, about a week or so later, he called me and asked me to help him with this cover. That was the first thing that I started doing with him for Depeche.

We helped sort out the design of the whole package.

He painted this piece of artwork and he had taken some photos in Milan, so really it was just a matter of helping him put it all together, and design the whole thing.

Back in those days, there were a plethora of different formats to make and then you know advertising and blah, blah, blah.

What that essentially meant was that he handed over those basic assets to us and then we helped put it all together and then designed the packaging for every sort of format and all the advertising, working with the record company.

He created all those pieces for 'Personal Jesus': the lettering and the painting of the cross.

I seem to remember that one of the challenges we had with that was working across multiple formats because everything had to be locked in.

It wasn't like we could move things around, so that was a bit of an issue initially for 'Violator', but fast-forward to 'Songs Of Faith And Devotion', we would ask him to make an alphabet for us and then we would create a typeface, which enabled us to make merchandising using the lettering and anything else we wanted to.

We had Anton write Depeche Mode in bold as our typeface and we were able to manipulate it. If we wanted to have the album title bigger, we could do that.

We didn't have to do any sort of cut-and-paste job. It was much easier. But that was sort of how that worked.

I don't remember specifically what was the motivation for the 'Personal Jesus' cover, but I think he was playing off of Martin Gore's obsession with religion and sex and all those sorts of things. Back then, pretty much every song Martin wrote about was some sort of nod to that.

Anton just had a simple idea: "'Personal Jesus'? Let's paint a cross!" So, okay, that is the idea. It wasn't about overthinking it. It was just about doing it.

Anton's personal approach to things – which I sort of adhered to – was that he is an amazing photographer but he isn't a fine artist... but he didn't necessarily realise this. He believed that what he created was good enough to put out there.

But that is kind of what it really takes, just to have an idea, create it and make it and put it on the cover of a record – and so he had a very simple approach to that sort of work.

It is funny because it is a little bit different to his photo style, which is really kind of moody and captures the real character of people. Still, Anton is a funny sort of guy and he likes to make silly jokes and stuff.

I believe he was inspired a little by Captain Beefheart / Don Van Vliet, who was also a painter and someone he had photographed.

If you look at Beefheart's paintings, there was always a similarity, so I feel there was some sort of influence there.

***

We didn't do a lot of presenting to the record label.

Anton would have maybe discussed with the band what he was thinking, perhaps show them a few sorts of things and then we would sort of doing it.

Even though that was pretty early in their relationship with him, they trusted him implicitly. And the record label was very hands-off – that was just the style of how it was in those days at least.

From that point on, for the next ten years, we did everything.

Initially, that started with all the singles, all of which came out around 'Violator' and all the merchandise, pretty much anything.

We didn't know at the beginning it was going to entail all the other elements, all the singles, the album cover and the merchandise.

The next single came along ('Enjoy The Silence') and we did that; the next single came along ('Policy Of Truth') and we did that too.

And then the album came along and we did that, and then merchandising needed to be done. The advertising needed to be done. The management company needed some stationary, so it just sort of happened.

It's very different to today where I think things are just sort of orchestrated and formal. It was very organic I think.

But, still, it worked out well with 'Personal Jesus' and 'Enjoy The Silence' and, by then, Anton relinquished a little bit of control.

We had more input in terms of putting the pieces together and deciding what we should do for the 12-inch and the 7-inch, so we decided to sort things with just the two of us: Anton and Area.

As we grew more familiar and confident with each other, he gave us more freedom.

It was definitely us at Area playing a bigger hand in making those decisions.

With 'Personal Jesus' there is an irony, in that it was really my first record cover even though I had worked for Peter Saville for four years.

When I was at Peter's, I only really formatted things. Yet to format something for a CD for a twenty-something New Order fan was amazing, so I didn't really care as I was just reformatting something.

So as things evolved with Anton and Depeche, I got more confident so by the time we got to 'Enjoy The Silence', Anton was giving us more freedom.

Record design was great back then – you could just mix it up and do whatever you wanted. For me the penny really dropped with the second single – we could do this, we could do that, we could shake things up in terms of different formats.

So we definitely got our wind with 'Enjoy The Silence'.

Also, 'Enjoy The Silence' was the direct connection to the album that followed.

'Violator' has the cut rose on the sleeve, which was a very subtle way of showing that it's this very beautiful, very delicate thing that has been violated, as it were.

So 'Enjoy The Silence' was our way of connecting to that whole package from a conceptual point of view.

***

I remember there being a lot of discussion around the title of the album – and I know Anton wasn't a big fan of it.

It was something to the effect that in other languages it meant rape or something like that.

I think he was concerned about the connotations of that. But those concerns didn't really stick. I definitely remember that was one thing.

He showed me the rose and explained his thought process behind it – about a delicate sort of object, violated, so it was a very subtle and simple nod to the title of the album.

It's painted red and it then has this kind of subtle reference to some sort of violation in a more gothic way, I suppose.

The rest of the package was just me trying to sort of put my mark on my first album cover and exploring ways of treating the typography and the lyrics and using the photography.

But, again, there was nothing contrived about the way it came together. It wasn't over-thought.

The rose is symbolic of love and femininity, to a certain extent, and so there we are coming back to Martin's obsession with sex and sexuality and the female.

And so that's why I think Anton was a little bit opposed to the title, as you could say it was some sort of S&M type of reference. But knowing Martin, and all of his kind of characteristics and loves and obsessions, it's a really subtle reference to all of that.

The rose is metaphorical in many ways to those things – love, affection, tenderness but also treating you like crap or S&M.

It is a very loaded image. That's only my interpretation of it all, but I'm sure that was a lot to do with it.

***

Up until the design phase of 'Violator', I'd had no direct contact with the band or heard any of the songs from the album.

Then I started to interact with them – I had to talk to Martin about what I was thinking of doing with the lyrics and some other simple stuff.

But I never got a pre-release tape or anything like that! I had no notion of what they were doing.

In fact, I wasn't even a big fan. I was a big fan in my teens when they had done things like 'Just Can't Get Enough', but I lost interest. I think a lot of people lost faith in them a little bit through the 1980s.

But this actually rekindled my interest in them.

Still, none of them really minced their words, so they were different from a lot of musicians, in that if they didn't like something, they would tell you. Of all the musicians I ever worked for, they were the most successful and were clearly going to become even more successful – so you listened to them!

But there were no challenges or anything. Again, they were happy just to hand it all off. They didn't meddle or micro-manage.

They put all their faith in Anton, and I was really under Anton's wing. So if Anton said it was okay, they said it was okay.

Anton was the creative force, so there was no day-to-day, "Dave thinks this," or "Martin thinks this," or "Fletch likes this."

We just did it. They had put all their faith in Anton.

It's interesting though, I never got any feedback from the record company for any of the work.

I think Depeche and Anton and the management company were in charge – they were on one of those no-contract relationships with the record company.

They probably didn't give a fuck what the record company said. It was typical of most bands around that time.

***

By the time we got to 'Policy Of Truth' and 'World In My Eyes', I'm assuming Anton had gotten busier than he usually was and didn't have as much time.

'Policy Of Truth' was interesting because I remember him telling me, "I'm thinking of trying this new colour photo style and I'm going to photograph it using a torch or something."

I forget exactly how he did it but it was a massive move for him, the whole colour photo approach because he was obviously known as a black and white photographer for a long time.

He introduced me to a fashion designer at the same time who he had shot a whole bunch of photographs for in a very similar style to 'Policy Of Truth'.

He was moving on from the work he had been doing, but photography was definitely something that came easier to him.

The different colours he used for the different formats for the single were mostly done in the photography.

At this point I believe, he started to work with a dark room called BDI in London, which is run by Brian Dowling who was well known for working with fashion photographer Nick Knight.

All the big English photographers that started doing colour photography had worked with Dowling.

Some of the colours were done in the photographic printing process, but I know a lot of it was also shot like this.

There was a thing that started in the late-1980s and early 1990s, called cross-processing, which is developing negatives as transparencies.

What it does is it suddenly makes the colours look super vibrant. It's now an Instagram filter! But back then everybody was doing photographs that were with super-high and bright colours.

With 'World In My Eyes', Anton shot all the photos and we just decided which ones worked best with which format. There was no, "We want Fletch on this," or "Let's have Dave on this." It was just what worked best.

***

I think one of my favourites, from an execution point of view, is one of the 12-inch designs for 'Enjoy The Silence' – the D and M, with the orange rose in the middle and the small typography off to the side.

Still, I think the whole 'Enjoy The Silence' project was really successful from a design and visual point of view.

With 'Personal Jesus', Anton had painted a square with everything on it and that didn't allow us much room to manipulate any of the elements for different formats.

Whereas, with 'Enjoy The Silence', we had much more control over how every aspect came together. From my perspective and from a design perspective, this was more rewarding.

***

It's not just for 'Violator', as it's true for any album cover, but the best album covers just work.

People like Peter Saville didn't go in, thinking to themselves, "I want a picture of a gravestone on the cover of 'Love Will Tear Us Part' because Ian Curtis of Joy Division is going to die."

Similarly, 'Violator' was just representative of an idea.

This is from a philosophical point of view that I believe in a lot, which is that you create it, you make it, you put it out there, and people then give it meaning.

You don't need to think about it too much. It's like an artist puts an upside-down symbol in the middle of a gallery and people think it is one of the most groundbreaking pieces of work of art ever because he made it, put it out there and people gave it meaning.

Record covers are symbols of people's adoration for the band. They become more than iconic.

I remember when I was at college, I was really into record cover design and one of the projects we were given was to redesign a record cover.

I remember looking at some of my colleagues' work and so many of them tried to interpret the title of the album or single through the visual and usually those kinds of album covers don't work.

That's why with 'Violator', somehow, it just makes sense. There weren't a lot of days of thought and conceptualising and deliberation over options and variations.

It was just that Anton said, "I think there should be a red rose on the cover and should be cut because it symbolises X", and so he did it, and made it, and we put it out there, and people attached all this meaning to it.

It works for the record. There's no true reflection of the song in one or any other way, but it works.

Today is the opposite of that – where everybody deliberates over every meaning and interpretation and what are people going to say, versus, "We like it, let's just do it."

***

I wasn't an avid fan so I didn't really have any sort of sense of their trajectory.

I knew Anton had come in and was sort of reinventing them a little bit, but it was only by working with them that I got to understand the enormity of who they were and, for example, the influence that they were said to have on house music in Detroit.

I didn't know any of that and I was sort of naive to that.

So I had no clue about the enormity of it all going into the project. It's only in retrospect that I have been able to sort of appreciate and realise that.

I obviously saw it later on, because the success that I directly received from that was people wanting to work for me and other musicians wanting me to work for them.

I worked for OMD, Tears For Fears and ABC, and all these big 1980s bands, just like Depeche Mode, who wanted to reinvent themselves... but who just weren't as talented.

Because I had worked with Depeche, they would call and say, "Hey, can you design me a record cover? We like what you did for Depeche Mode."

Depeche were in a similar boat up until that point, so they definitely did an about-face, yet they made it happen and they continued to grow.

I think about Roland Orzabal from Tears For Fears – his head definitely was bigger than what you could fit through a door. His ego was enormous because he was so successful.

And I remember, we were working on some crappy album for them and he was saying, "Everyone at the record company is really excited! This is going to be a big hit, this is going to be massive."

But this was all these sycophantic people that just kissed ass – yet Depeche weren't like that.

They didn't have to do that. You don't have to say you're good if you're good.

And whether that was because they were down to earth or they just hadn't been affected by it, I don't know. I think it was more that they were just very talented.

You look at how they have continued to produce good albums, time and time again, unlike OMD, Tears For Fears, unlike ABC, unlike anybody that generally was one of their contemporaries at that time.

There were hundreds of bands around when the Rolling Stones started and yet the Stones are still going on to this day. It's just how things shake out.

To me, it's just that they were really talented and they didn't have to tell anybody they were good. They just were good.

***

'Sticky Fingers' by the Rolling Stones is an iconic album cover. But it is indicative of a time and sort of idea of music and musicians and a visual style of that era.

That album captured something of that era, so you could argue that that is less timeless because of that, whereas 'Violator' is probably more timeless because it is just simple.

'Violator' is something of which I'm proud because of its success and, therefore, it's up there in terms of being one of the most successful covers I have ever worked on. And so I am really proud of that.

It's funny, this might just be a personal thing, but I think I want to be objective about it and not get tied up with personal attachments. I think I see it more as an outsider in the same way other people do, but then there is a subtle pride that that is something I did.

Still, especially in America, tell anybody you designed Depeche Mode's 'Violator' cover and they become like in Wayne's World, "I'm not worthy!"

Angela Shelton (USA), actress in the video for 'Clean'

I was most definitely a fan of Depeche Mode before I got to be in the 'Clean' video. I had been a fan since 'People Are People' and I was a huge 'Black Celebration' fan.

I went to a massive casting call full of models. I was sitting on the floor reading a book (I think Henry Miller) and the casting director thought I stood out more than the others due to that fact and spent more time with me.

We shot at the house in the hills for the pool and then shot on a sound stage for the sofa scene. There was more production of that required because of the video playing in the background.

I knew they were staying there but I didn't know it was their rented apartment. I think the shoot was two days.

Martin Gore was the only band member present. He was not there during the pool scene but obviously there on the sofa!

I was thrilled. I was actually dating an extremely jealous guy who flipped out when I told him, so I broke up with him to do the video.

I was a huge fan of Martin and was more than happy to make out with him, but we did the 'Hollywood' version where you don't actually touch tongues. Believe me, I tried. He was very professional and kind.

Anton was wonderful and everyone was very professional and kind. It was not like the horror stories you hear. In fact, I was the one who was lamenting the fact we weren't actually making out. I love Martin!

I was invited to see the tour after we filmed the video and got VIP backstage passes. It was fantastic. And I'm still a fan!

Pam Heffer (USA), dancer in the video for 'Halo'

I was dancing with a choreographer named Sarah Elgart in her dance company at the time and she recommended me to the director since she was choreographing the video.

I auditioned for the video and I suppose it was not long before we shot it.

I probably didn't know much about Depeche Mode... just their name!

I believe we only shot for one day and one evening. It could have been two but I don't remember exactly. I don't believe much was discussed about the concept of the video, just how we would participate.

We were shooting in the desert but I remember being sort of cold in our bikini-style outfits!

There was the choreographer and I believe most everything was done right on location, so very little rehearsal. We did hang out with the band and I remember everyone being super-cool and very easy going to work with.

I was actually surprised by the video – I didn't know it was going to be so unusual. What we did was super-goofy and pretty straight forward and the video is rather eclectic, creative and unusual in a great way!

What may be of interest is, back in the day, we got very little money for music videos and they were all done 'non-union', so I never saw any footage of this until rather recently, which was the case for almost everything I danced in back then.

I believe the world of dance is now much more protected by the union [now], or at least I hope it is!

Michael Rose (UK), fan and collector

Caroline Rose (France), fan

Michael Rose, fan and collector

When I think back on the 'Violator' era, I can't help but remember the anticipation ahead of the album's release.

In August 1989, 'Personal Jesus' was released, our first taste of the new album. After the excitement of the teaser advertising campaign, in true Depeche Mode-style, we were hit with a new sound and direction, a mix of blues and electronica with loads of guitar. Among the collection of remixes, we even got an acoustic version!

When 'Enjoy The Silence' followed in February 1990, I was completely blown away. It was quite simply one of the best things I'd heard by anyone, ever.

To this day, it's still capable of giving me goosebumps and remains one of my favourite Depeche Mode tracks. It was more what you would expect from Depeche Mode, and its mass appeal was clear, giving the band their highest UK chart position since 1984.

Quite something when you think of the quality of 'Black Celebration' and 'Music For The Masses', and the singles they produced.

And then, of course, there were the release formats and the artwork.

As a collector, this was adding to the excitement as much as the new music. Along with the usual 7-inch, 12-inch, limited 12-inch, CD and limited CD, 'Personal Jesus' was also released in a gatefold sleeve 7-inch single, a first for Depeche Mode.

With 'Enjoy The Silence', we were treated to a third 12-inch and CD, with a glorious 15-minute mix of the single, with an etching on the vinyl version. The artwork, now in the hands of Anton Corbijn, along with the album cover we had yet to see, was to become iconic.

March 19, 1990, and the wait was over, 'Violator' was released. From the simple, yet striking and beautiful image of a red rose on a black background, at complete odds with the hard and aggressive connotations of the word 'Violator', to the first listen from start to finish, it was a complete experience to be immersed in.

It was a masterpiece, perfect, there wasn't a single track I didn't love on first listen.

From the opening notes of 'World In My Eyes', to the hypnotic fading out of 'Clean', it had my complete, undivided attention. The band had grown and matured, there was confidence in the album, and the sound was polished and flawless.

Dave's vocal range had improved, showcased perfectly on the gorgeous 'Waiting For The Night'. There seemed to be so many potential singles, too – 'Halo' being a standout track.

I don't remember how many times I listened to it in that first sitting, but it was the only album I played for quite some time, it went with me everywhere. My only disappointment with the album was that there were only nine tracks, two of which we'd had prior to release.

In getting only seven new tracks, I felt cheated. I wanted more! We did of course have a great collection of B-sides, and the single releases continued.

Ahead of the 'World Violation Tour' starting in the US, 'Policy Of Truth' was released in May 1990, and prior to the tour arriving in Europe, 'World In My Eyes' came in September.

A slick release schedule, whip up a frenzy before hitting us with the live shows!

The release formats for these singles continued to impress. 'Policy Of Truth' gave us a gatefold sleeve 12-inch single, while 'World In My Eyes' was available in a limited-edition 12-inch single that came in a blue sealed plastic sleeve, with instructions to "violate here" in order to access the aural delights inside.

After only instrumentals that backed the previous two singles, 'World In My Eyes' was released with two new tracks, a great way to push the fourth single from a nine-track album.

I didn't care, they were brilliant and I'd have bought it anyway, such was my devotion at the time. Over the following years, my collection of 'Violator'-related items has risen to over 100, including 27 different copies of the album itself.

Funnily enough, my passion and obsession with Depeche Mode were now being understood a little more by people around me.

Having been ridiculed for being a fan back in the 1980s, my tormentors were now taking Depeche Mode more seriously. I had championed the band for years, encouraging people to go and see them in concert, forgetting their preconceived ideas, and they were coming around.

The success of 'Music For The Masses' and the tour that followed had really paved the way for a much warmer reception to 'Violator' as we entered a new decade. The proof was there, in the album achieving their highest UK chart position to date.

Next on the agenda, was of course seeing the band live on the 'World Violation Tour'.

For this tour, I had vowed to myself that I would go to every UK date they played. Having travelled to Germany to see them on the last tour, how could I possibly sit at home in London knowing they were playing somewhere else in England?

Luckily, the 'Music For The Masses Tour' was the last time they actually toured the UK, playing in cities up and down the country. This time, the fans were going to have to go to them, no longer would they be playing more intimate theatres and the like.

Just two UK dates were initially announced, London and Birmingham, in November 1990. Once these were sold out, a second date was added to each venue, and eventually a third. Six dates in two cities, this UK tour was going to be easy, and tickets were secured for all of the shows.

Not satisfied with this, I made plans to see them live in Europe again. For this tour, I decided on Paris, and tickets were booked for two nights at the Palais Omnisports de Paris-Bercy in October, ahead of the UK shows.

All eight shows I attended were outstanding, witnessing this magnificent album come to life in a live setting. The Paris shows, though, were a notch above.

As well as being a fantastic venue, the passion of the French audience was something to behold and, just like in Germany, really showed the difference in how the band were perceived in Europe compared to the UK.

I'm not alone, and I think this is a huge factor in what makes UK fans travel far and wide to see Depeche Mode in concert. It's made even easier nowadays, with the internet and cheap travel. Back then, it was an adventure, trying to secure tickets for a gig in a foreign country and working out how you were going to get there, as cheaply as possible. Coaches, boats and trains made for some interesting journeys.

Here we are over 30 years later, and 'Violator' is still hailed as a masterpiece and remains the favourite album of many Depeche Mode fans.

It truly has stood the test of time; a genuine, *bona fide*, classic, timeless album. It still sounds as powerful and relevant today as it did all those years ago, an album I've never stopped listening to.

It represents Depeche Mode at the peak of their power when everything came together perfectly. The songs, the way they were shaped, the production, the artwork, the associated videos, and the live shows, it was an amazing time to be a Depeche Mode fan.

***

Caroline Rose, fan

The year that 'Violator' came out saw me live on both sides of the English Channel.

I was born and grew up in a small coastal town in the South of France and was completing my degree at the nearby University of Montpellier.

I had always enjoyed Depeche Mode among other New Wave/New Romantic bands of the time and also got seriously involved in heavy metal for a while.

I only became a real fan from 'Black Celebration' onwards. It was almost like suddenly, out of nowhere, some music satisfied my craving for darkness. There had been Roxy Music, but Depeche brought something else that seemed to feed me and reach deep inside, where no other music had ever reached before. It is difficult to put into words.

Then 'Music For The Masses' came along and my fate was sealed. From this point on, I have bought each single DM album systematically, ignoring reviews or opinions, just safe in the knowledge my craving was going to be satisfied somehow.

I had enjoyed the singles but nothing prepared me for my first listen to 'Violator'. I clearly remember the day. I took the bus into town from the hall of residents and queued at the FNAC to buy my copy of the much-awaited Violator.

On the ride back, I was ridden with excitement, clutching the little brown FNAC bag.

As an impoverished student on a grant, all I had in my humble dwellings was a portable CD / cassette player, which is where I had the first of many listens, on loop.

I lay on my single bed, eyes shut, and the adventure began. I was literally taken on a trip from the opening of 'World in My Eyes'.

Dave's voice gripped me. It was like being under a spell. It touched my soul. There was, and is something totally hypnotic about 'Violator' as a whole and the tone is set by this iconic opening track.

My response to music is a very emotional one, music speaks to me or doesn't. It is almost visceral and certainly not cerebral.

As a young 21-year-old, I was stirred in more ways than one and started developing an obsession with the music and the band.

'Violator' was on loop in my student room and as summer came I began to turn the volume up with the window open, perhaps subconsciously hoping to "spread the news" or that someone would knock on my door wanting to talk about this incredible music.

I have always found that there was something deeply sexual about most of the tracks but in a subtle way. Martin Gore has always explored relationships from this unusual angle of devotion mixed with sex and it goes without saying that at 21, I found it fascinating and often sat in wonder, yearning to experience such a relationship. This was severely heightened with 'Songs Of Faith And Devotion' in 1993, but that is another story… Back to 'Violator': 'Halo' was another powerful track for me as was 'Policy of Truth'.

But anyway, fast forward to September 1990. I have left my digs in Montpellier and am now in a shared house in Coventry,

UK, working as a French Assistant while doing a Masters Degree.

Suddenly, I had an income, albeit a modest one, total freedom and I was in the land of music, HMV, cool bands etc… The wind was about to turn!

The release of the 'World In My Eyes' single with 'Sea Of Sin' and 'Happiest Girl' took me further into my addiction to DM. I totally fell in love with these two tracks and still fail to understand to this day why they were B-sides and why they have never been played live by the band.

They are everything 'Violator' is about, and more. They are dark and upbeat all at once, intriguing and they went straight to my heart. I know many fans feel the same about them and they remain some of my all-time favourites.

I was exploring the town one day shortly after arriving and happened to walk past a record shop, the kind we don't find anymore these days, advertising the last few remaining tickets for Depeche Mode at the NEC in November.

My heart skipped a beat and without even worrying about whether I would find someone to go with me I walked in and bought a ticket.

This has to be one of the most exciting music-related moments in my life.

I have to put it in context: I didn't grow up in cool London or anywhere near it. I was a small-town French girl with next to no money, in a culture where you did not get a Saturday job to pay for your passions.

I had so little that I only bought LPs around Christmas and my birthday, the occasional single with my pocket money and most of my music was taped from friends' LPs or the radio, or even off the TV! That's all there was and I was used to it.

The same went for gigs: although music was always a huge part of my life and I hung around local bands and attended local gigs, the patriarchal society in which I lived meant that a young girl did not go on her own to big rock gigs.

I saw a few shows with my mum at the Zenith, French bands and singers such as Étienne Daho, for example, but my first stadium gig was an 18th birthday present. No coolitude here.

So, yes, I was a DM gig virgin. As it turned out, my job involved teaching French to some Sixth Form students, who were only a few years younger and happened to be DM fans too, so we all went together to the NEC. And 'Violated' we were!!

It felt more like a giant mass than a gig to me, the intensity was out of this world and Dave had us all in the palm of his hand. Again, this spell feeling came over me.

I remember thinking that if at some point he had asked the audience to set the place on fire or do something silly, we would have done it. It was like being part of some sort of cult.

At the gig, I bought an oversized t-shirt and giant posters, as well as the programme. I slept with the t-shirt over my pyjamas for days. My obsession was fuelled further after this first live experience and I could think of little else for a long time. I have not felt this so strongly again at any of their other gigs, but then I missed the whole 'SOFAD' tour, so what do I know…

Life took over eventually and I had to return to normality but DM remained with me every step of the way for the rest of my time in the UK.

I believe that although 'Black Celebration' was the album that made me a fan, and 'SOFAD' is my favourite, 'Violator' is definitely the one that made me turn a corner as a fan. It sealed my addiction to their music, I totally embraced their depth and darkness and to this day I can't think of any band who can satisfy this need in me in the way they do, so totally and unconditionally.

Chapter 5

Heights Of Sounds And Songs

"I think that we were aware that we were making a record that was exciting. I have very fond memories of making 'Violator', on every level - the partying had hit an all-time high, the experimentation, the excitement in the studio, the songs. But I don't think we were really aware of what was going on in terms of people waiting for this record and what was about to explode."

***

'Violator' was released on Monday, March 19, 1990.

The album had been recorded in around four months and two singles had preceded its unveiling, with 'Personal Jesus' and 'Enjoy The Silence' coming out in August 1989 and February 1990 respectively.

Fewer than two years had passed since the Pasadena Rose Bowl gig in June 1988 but there had been a seismic shift in the attitude and an enthusiasm for change in the band during the intervening period.

There were changes in the wider music industry at the same time, too, with the emergence of house music as a genre and the controversial arrival of rave culture in the UK.

Everything was changing, including in the band, with Dave Gahan's marriage facing some difficulties and other members beginning to experience their own challenges with mental health and the beginnings of alcohol problems.

The 1980s had been a rollercoaster of a ride so far and, at the time of 'Violator's release, only one band member, Alan Wilder, was in his 30s.

Many of the aforementioned problems would manifest themselves in different ways in the years to come, not least Gahan's eventual addiction to heroin, but for the time being this now well-established band, with its four young band members, had the world at their feet.

They didn't quite realise it though.

The two singles had done well upon their release, especially 'Enjoy The Silence'. 'Personal Jesus' had laid the groundwork that the new Depeche Mode was not one that people would instantly recognise, both sonically and visually.

It reached number 28 on the US Billboard Hot 100 charts, competing with the likes of chart leaders Paula Abdul, New Kids On The Block and Gloria Estefan during the month of September.

On the band's home turf, British fans got the single to number 13 in the Top 40 Singles Chart, with Germany scoring the fifth spot, third in Italy and Spain, and a surprisingly low number 27 in France.

'Enjoy The Silence', with its quirky video and poppier sensibilities, reached the top of the charts in Spain and Denmark, the sixth position in the UK, second in Germany and ninth in France.

Crucially for what was to come, the second single marked a lofty eighth spot on the Billboard Hot 100 chart.

Billboard's Alternative Airplay chart, an important indicator of what the US college circuit and non-mainstream radio stations were playing, saw 'Personal Jesus' and 'Enjoy The Silence' in third and first positions.

Depeche Mode had performed consistently well in the mainstream European charts throughout the 1980s. Chart positions are one thing, but 'Violator's aesthetic and a combination of electronic and organic instrumentation meant that the critics were starting to take notice, too.

The feeling in the band and the wider Depeche Mode camp at Mute at the time was one of acknowledging an extremely strong piece of work. Flood and Daniel Miller had, in the 'Violator' producer's words, exchanged expressions at one another after the album's first playback session in London in the early autumn of 1989, which indicated that they realised things were going to be big this time on the back of a creative *tour de force*.

***

There was obviously a tremendous amount of work that had gone into the production of the album, including the seismic leap in techniques and approach taken to dissect and record the tracks – but this was not just a four-month period in studios in Italy, Denmark and the UK.

Martin Gore's songs were the culmination of a still relatively short lifetime of experiences – an element of the creative process that is not often recognised or appreciated.

Many of the tracks on the album were considered some of the best that he'd ever written by his fellow band members and the close-knit circle of assistants and crew members.

The crucial forces of mature, creative songwriting and new production techniques – at least in terms of how tracks were approached – had aligned perfectly.

The new studio set-up of Flood, coupled with his burgeoning creative relationship with Alan Wilder, had been introduced at the perfect time for Depeche Mode, giving Gore's songs a chance to breathe and take on a new life.

'Violator' was cinematic, edgy, dark, light and extremely forward-looking in terms of sound. No other electronic band had made a record quite like 'Violator'.

The album's release in March 1990, warmly anticipated by fans and undoubtedly fuelled by many curious newcomers after the release of 'Enjoy The Silence', saw the 47-minute collection of songs hit the number one spot in Spain, Greece, France and Belgium.

It eventually reached number two in the UK, Switzerland and Germany, number four in Austria, fifth spot in Canada, sixth in Sweden and Italy and US Billboard 200 placed it at number seven.

The first week that 'Violator' was featured in the US charts in position 43, leading spots one to five featured Bonnie Raitt, Paula Abdul, Janet Jackson, Michael Bolton and Alannah Myles.

By its second week, 'Violator' was in position 14, tenth a week later and seventh by the first week of May. It was a tremendous achievement and a signal that the album had been both extremely well-received and the forthcoming massive tour across the US, including three huge shows in Los Angeles and New York, was an accurate forecast of how popular the band had become.

Somewhat predictably, given how Depeche Mode were still often treated with disdain or mild bemusement by so-called serious music critics, reviews were fairly split on 'Violator's initial release.

The UK's 'Q' magazine gave the album four out of five, claiming that "the music remains neither particularly upbeat nor commercial, yet it's full of insidious songs that creep up on you and hug the brain with distressing tenacity.

"Yet this is not so much an album of doom and gloom as a seductive sharing of openness and intimacy… Creative but disciplined and always interesting… 'Violator' is a fine record which may not set the world on fire but deserves to singe it a bit."

Fellow British music magazine 'Smash Hits', which generally focused on the poppier end of the market but had covered Depeche Mode for throughout the 1980s, wrote that the band "carry on making the same strange records that pay not the blindest bit of notice to what the rest of pop music sounds like."

Its eight out of ten review said 'Violator' was "hypnotically addictive and… rather fab."

The British music press appeared to have woken up – finally – to Depeche Mode, or at least had decided they were no longer to be the whipping boys when critics were looking to practice their wit and clever words via their sharp pens.

Another, 'Record Mirror', gave 'Violator' a strong four out of five, somewhat amusingly proclaiming "after years of trying, Depeche Mode have finally succeeded in making 'The Black Album'… with 'Violator', they have fashioned a veritable dungeon of songs for you to jangle your manacles to.

"There are no noises out of place in this perfectly formed void. The songs are like bright stars in a black sky or silver studs on a soft black leather jacket. The wonder is the more they strip it down the bigger they get. How low can they go?"

Curiously, stateside, critics were less favourable in their analysis of the new long-player, with 'Rolling Stone' writing: "The group has been single-mindedly suffocating in Doorsy depression ever since songsmith Vince Clarke left for Yazoo."

Oddly, despite the obvious maturity and development of the band's sound over the proceeding nine years, 'Rolling Stone' lamented how Depeche Mode would "never again make a number as compelling as the 1981 gleeful rubber-duckie disco tune 'Just Can't Get Enough'."

The review continued, "Teens too old or too kinky for New Kids On The Block apparently find David Gahan's quavering moan sexy, but on 'Violator', he sometimes comes off as slimy and self-involved. Depeche Mode has got away with cute little mechanized blips, and the train whistles and raga rhythms and air traffic control signals put monotony on hold.

"Depeche Mode's more tranquil hymns do have an ambient charm. But when the boys in the band try to make you dance, they revert to morose pop psychology and then never tell you how come they're so sad."

The 'Los Angeles Times', combining a review of the album with reflections on a show at the beginning of the tour, wrote, "The heart of Depeche Mode's appeal is Gore's songs. While striking emotional chords, most lack a compelling literary or poetic edge. This makes them too easily absorbed, all but forcing the more demanding members of Depeche Mode's mainstream pop-rock audience to move on to the more artful and demanding sounds of U2 and the Cure, among rival stadium attractions.

"The challenge for Depeche Mode is to grow with its young audience. While that may be difficult for a group about to enter its second decade, there are signs of growth in the 'Violator album.

"Regardless of its eventual fate, Depeche Mode's success is a sign of change in the rock world at large and that's good. How ironic that a band so associated with angst could serve as such an encouraging sign of hope."

'Entertainment Weekly' described Depeche Mode, for some as "pop kings; for others, they're too vapid, too mechanized, or too pompous."

It continued, "Their music is more varied than catchy pop needs to be. 'World In My Eyes', the opening track, begins with music that sounds like some ungainly cartoon animal dancing. The second song, 'Sweetest Perfection', starts low, then quickly adds something high and eerie, like the keening of a thousand tiny neon gnats.

"None of these distinctive and curious effects (there must be dozens of them) interferes with the easy flow of the music.

Sometimes, though, they do cast shadows, the significance of which can be hard to figure out. These shadows in effect hint at unspecified meanings, in a mannered way that might well be called pompous — until one song, 'Halo', opens a window on what the band might really be about. 'You wear guilt like shackles on your feet, like a halo in reverse,' the lyrics say, while the music dances darkly.

"This emotional sickness – 'a famine in your heart' – is captured by harmonies that float over the music as if they were the disturbing odour of slowly rotting fruit. Even 'Waiting For The Night', on its surface a song about tranquillity, drifts on a sea of unease. There's a worm eating at Depeche Mode's gut. Maybe at heart, they're not wholly pop."

Back in the UK, 'NME' – the weekly music paper that was notorious for building up and knocking down bands and / or genres with carefree ease, said that 'Violator' "seems almost a step back, in that it's cleaner, sparser, more clinical.

"There is security in the knowledge that everything is very clear cut in Depeche Mode's blue and white world."

A crucial element in the aftermath of 'Violator's release was that despite the mixed reviews, hardcore fans would've dismissed them anyway and simply enjoyed the new material and newer fans would have been curious enough to see what else the creators of the pre-album singles 'Personal Jesus' and 'Enjoy The Silence' could do.

Neither group of people would've cared for music critics who may have been eagerly sharpening their pens ahead of any new release, such as how the band were still considered by those who were paid to give their opinions as somewhat lightweight and lacking in direction.

What is perhaps most interesting about the reaction to 'Violator', aside from a few negative reviews, was that it was almost universally agreed – outside of the critic bubble that Depeche Mode had created – an arresting, exciting, deep and career-defining volume of new material.

Both Andy Fletcher – provider of the title of this chapter, from a Q&A discussion in 2003 to mark the re-release of the '101' movie – and Martin Gore have since stated that 'Violator' is their favourite Depeche Mode album.

Alan Wilder, when quitting the band in 1995 and interviews since has said the final two albums that he worked on, both with Flood, were illustrations of where the band was heading.

"My decision to leave the group was not an easy one particularly as our last few albums were an indication of the full potential that Depeche Mode was realising," he wrote in a statement to announce his departure in 1995.

One evergreen piece of commentary that is cited regarding 'Violator' is its timeless and fresh sound, even years later. This was the point that many had been making back in 1990.

This was no more apparent in the reviews that accompanied its re-release in 2006, where the passage of time had given 'Violator' the respect that it undoubtedly deserved.

'The Guardian' newspaper in the UK wrote, "Violator, the pick of three new DVD-bolstered remasters, wasn't just

Depeche Mode's biggest album, cementing their status as the world's first electronic stadium stars and prompting a riot at an LA record signing. It was also their best, encasing Martin Gore's favourite tropes – guilt, salvation, obsession and the virtues of keeping your mouth shut – in production as black and shiny as a beetle's shell.

"'Personal Jesus"'s lusty glam-blues stomp is a red herring; most of the time 'Violator' moves with bewitching stealth, from the smouldering electro of 'World In My Eyes' to the eerie catharsis of 'Clean', the lyrics of which acquired a gloss of irony when Dave Gahan later plunged into heroin addiction. The DVD features a making-of documentary and six iPod-unfriendly bonus tracks, but this nocturnal masterpiece requires no embellishment."

Online music magazine 'Pitchfork' said, "Like any good crossover, this record needs no particular context to appreciate and listening back through, one gets a sense of why: The battle they're winning here, of giving electronic music the human feel of teenage anthems and power ballads, is the same one still being fought by any number of Germans; it's not constrained by time. The dark and slinky soul of the record – the sex or drama-queen poses, the mix of domineering threats and extreme tenderness – don't hurt either."

'Slant' had also written, "Depeche Mode's 'Violator' is a quintessential benchmark of pop, rock, and electronic music, seamlessly marrying dance, goth-rock, and synth-pop with good ol' fashioned funk and rock 'n' roll. In fact, it could be said that 'Violator' violated the standard definition of popular music itself.

"Gore intertwines sex and addiction on the dirgy 'The Sweetest Perfection' and then again on the cinematic final track, 'Clean'. 'Blue Dress' – an electronic swing number, if you will – is at once profoundly sad, sexy, and creepy, as Gore croons 'put it on' (referring to the titular dress) repeatedly throughout. 'Something so worthless serves a purpose,' he sings. 'It makes me a happy man'.

"When Gahan takes the mic, it's hard to believe he didn't write the words coming out of his mouth: 'You wear guilt…like a halo in reverse,' he sings on 'Halo'. The countermelody of the song's last few moments hints at 'Policy Of Truth', which presents itself fully a few tracks later. The theme of lies and consequence continue, but this time Gahan / Gore is less compassionate than he is outright jaded: 'You'll see your problems multiplied / If you continually decide / To faithfully pursue / The policy of truth.' The band would go on to construct even more stylistically diverse collections of songs (2001's under-appreciated 'Exciter', which vaguely echoes 'Violator'), but no other Depeche Mode album has been this captivating or sophisticated."

The world of online media and review sites has allowed for some aggregation of fan feedback, giving the chance to see what the wider support and praise for 'Violator' have been over the years.

Review platform 'RateYourMusic' has 'Violator' at third in its list of albums from 1990 and an extremely respectable 152 overall.

'Billboard' summarised 'Violator' turning 25 in 2015 by writing, "The Mode's stellar seventh album was, in some ways, an unlikely pop smash. For years, songwriter, and musical mastermind Martin Gore had been exploring religion and kinky sex, and on 'Violator', he keeps on going.

"Gore name-checks Jesus on the lead single and ponders obsessive desire on most of the other eight tracks. This wasn't exactly stuff Paula Abdul or New Kids On The Block were singing about at the time."

And 'Albumism', to coincide with 30 years since its release, said, "For a band that is often slighted by being dour, dark and depressive in their sound, 'Violator', for the most part, is quite an uplifting and optimistic album. Sure there is a celebration of carnal desires, but as it shows in the bouncy pop-oriented 'Policy Of Truth' the darker side of love can be presented in almost joyous tones.

"With 'Violator', Depeche Mode boldly pushed their sound into the new decade. With each ensuing release, they would continue to push and explore. But here, on 'Violator', they are at their most ambitious and focused.

"They found a way to be epic in their production yet remain intimate in how their songs connect with the listener. It was an album well worth the wait, and remains one still wildly enjoyable today."

Gareth Jones (UK), producer, mixer and engineer for Depeche Mode 1983 to 1986, 1997 and 2001

I don't know if the songwriting is darker on 'Songs Of Faith And Devotion' ('SOFAD') than it is on 'Violator'.

It's interesting because the album titles are inverse to how we describe them. 'Violator', that's pretty dark. Violation isn't something most people look for.

It's not, "I'm going to go out and get violated". Violation seems like a brutal assault. It's interesting – maybe this is Martin and the band having fun with wordplay and flipping around the inherent emotions of the album.

But in a way, we didn't know that 'SOFAD' was coming. So in the context of what 'Violator' was in 1989 and 1990, 'SOFAD' wasn't even on our horizon as listeners or fans. I get what Flood has said about 'Violator' and 'SOFAD' reflecting the moments in time of the band, of course, because the band have got very catholic and eclectic musical tastes. So I'm sure the rock and the live drum elements of 'SOFAD' are just as close to their hearts as the pure electronic nature of 'Violator'.

How wonderfully fulfilling to be able to express two sides of your musical personality in two albums so close together. I'm sure they have got other sides to their personality as well!

Music lovers of their age now, genuine music lovers, have kind of embraced the wealth of different musical genres out there, not just electronic pop or doomy rock or whatever 'SOFAD' was.

There is obviously a famous electric guitar riff on 'Personal Jesus'. I remember the multi-tracks and track sheets of the songs of the Berlin Trilogy that I worked on with them

– 'Construction Time Again', 'Some Great Reward', and 'Black Celebration'. I was astonished to see, in retrospect, how many acoustic instruments were on there, and how many samples of acoustic instruments there were as well. Because I had gone along with the popular mythology that the 'non-synthesisers' stage came later but I don't think it did.

Obviously, 'Just Can't Get Enough' is pure synthesisers. I certainly thought of 'Violator' as this supremely accomplished electronic music album when it arrived. It seemed to me like Depeche's take on Kraftwerk.

And obviously the choice of having François Kevokian mix the record reflected that as well. Because he had just done 'Electric Cafe' with Kraftwerk, before he did 'Violator'. So his aesthetic is tying those two records together as well.

It seemed to me that it was very streamlined, very focused. I had a huge admiration for the band and for Flood when they came up with that record because Flood had already done U2's 'Joshua Tree', so when he stepped up and produced 'Violator' I was very impressed.

But, of course, it's not just Flood; he was part of the record and I was impressed by the band and the whole production team. Alan, obviously, and Martin.

Certainly, Alan was very involved in the production side. And when I first met him back in 1982, he was very interested in production. Martin now is very interested in it and maybe that was the start!

So there are masses of great talent working on the record – it's all so well-honed, like a great piece of architecture. It doesn't seem overladen – it's not minimal but there's nothing superfluous to it.

It's very focused. So it's kind of gleaming and machine-like. It totally absorbed the spirit of Kraftwerk and made it their own. But because the songwriting is different, the soul sensibility of the vocal is very different.

They demonstrated their own pretty clearly when making the next album so that they wouldn't be pigeonholed. I think that's one of the things that I've admired about them and I love about artists, in general, is when they try new stuff.

A part of being creative is trying new things. Picasso didn't stay in his blue period his whole life, he drew on that and then similarly, his whole cubist phase he moved on later, but he drew on it and moved through different phases.

Many artists do it and Depeche belonged to that group of artists that try new stuff. And how radically were they doing it then, going from 'Black Celebration', 'Music For The Masses', 'Violator' and 'SOFAD' – pretty different sounding records.

***

I have a prejudiced view of 'Music For The Masses'. I'd made three records with them back-to-back and then they went off and started working with someone else.

I didn't have much time for it because I was no longer part of the team. So there was a sense that our paths had diverged. But at the time, as a younger man, I was a bit disappointed that when I made 'Black Celebration' with them that we didn't carry on working together.

But, hey, nothing lasts forever and we were all working many different creative and musical partnerships and it's great, but then I was like, "Oh, they have gone off to work with someone else!"

Having done three records, perhaps I had settled into a kind of comfortable presumption that we would carry on working together. And in fact, we did work together later in different areas and I had the pleasure of working with Mark Bell on 'Exciter' and I worked a tiny bit on 'Ultra' as well, so essentially our work relationship picked up again.

But after 'Black Celebration' I felt a bit abandoned, so I was a bit prejudiced about 'Music For The Masses' and didn't realise it to be the good album that it was.

By the time 'Violator' came along, enough water had passed under the bridge that I was able to embrace it and listen to it and enjoy it. It is the pinnacle of their career, isn't it?

It might be one of the finest albums – but how can you judge and say what the best record is possible? Every record is super important to the band.

It is a pinnacle perhaps, probably by sales. 'Personal Jesus' was a huge single. That alone is enough to flag it up because pop is all about reaching people, it's about extensive reach. That is the idea of pop art I think. So 'Personal Jesus' certainly did that. They cracked it and went to a new level globally.

'Enjoy The Silence' is another amazing single as well, another huge global single. So that was pretty incredible.

I think the album just seems to be incredibly well crafted. There's something about the architecture of the album, the way the instrumentation supports the vocals, the songwriting, the power of the album and the sound of the album, is very modern and contemporary and glossy, which is obviously the band, the producer, the engineers, the mixers, the whole thing.

Everything just kind of clicked. It's big but it's not clumsy. It's a big-sounding record but it's not fat – it's big and muscular. It's all very present.

It's not just eight months of songwriting – it's a lifetime. If you're 50 and you write a song and it takes you ten minutes, it's actually taken you 50 years.

It was awful that the main songwriter left the group in 1981. But clearly, it was the best thing that could have happened for Martin because then he was really super encouraged and had the space and inner resources to become the great songwriter he became.

And who knows if it would have been different, without that abandonment and without that trauma? We are very quick to judge, aren't we, as human beings? Something happens and we always go, this is good and that's bad. Something happens really badly but actually, obviously, the universe shows us time and time again that we might be wrong about our snap judgement.

There are wonderful stories like that. And this is one of them, the songwriting story.

Alan, too, was always super interested in the studio as an instrument and production. He was always in the studio, all the time.

Like an assistant, Daniel, me and Alan were in the studio all the time, for all those albums in the trilogy. Because he loved it. We all loved being in the studio.

But I think Martin and Dave and Fletch, initially, didn't perhaps love it as much. Obviously, they loved making records because they were an electropop band. But Alan was definitely a bit geekier at that time than the rest of the band. He was very interested in the technology and how it all worked and tape recording and mixing consoles and everything.

***

I can't remember where I first heard 'Personal Jesus'. I was still very close to Mute Records. They probably sent me a vinyl or something, because there was a time when record companies were making a lot more money, and they were more generous with giving out vinyl.

I was a bit of a staff producer for Mute, in some ways, I did a lot of records in the 1980s with them. And so they probably just sent me a record and said, "This is the new Depeche record!"

I probably heard it in my apartment in Berlin. I think, by the time that came out, I also had an amazing stereo because I had generated quite a lot of royalties working with Erasure and I spent a lot of money on an amazing stereo. That's probably also why I thought it was such a great-sounding record! It was beautifully done.

I'm sure by then no one was controlling them. I'm sure that's just what they wanted to do. I would be very surprised if, by the time they were that age, they were doing what anyone says. Why would you?

A successful 30-year-old footballer or rock group or pop group or any other artist, they are not going to do what someone else says.

Maybe Flood had had a conversation with them, as it was their first record with him. Maybe they had a meeting and agreed, "You know what? Let's do it like this. Let's show up for work." It kind of makes sense. I would do that if I worked with younger bands now.

I think Flood was partying with the band because he was young as well. I met that band in that period, where everybody is going out and drinking afterwards, really full-on. Anyway, we have all been young once and drunk a lot more than we do know probably and done a lot more drugs than we do now.

But let's make music when we are in the studio and we can go out afterwards.

They presented François with an album that he could mix the way that he did. François polished and honed it and chipped bits off it and made it really muscular and funky, but that's what they delivered to him.

As a mixer, you might choose to do something like mute all the electric guitars. And then say, "Look, guys, what do you think? I just listened to it without all the guitars. It's amazing!" and then everyone says, "Good job, great!".

Because he had come off the back of the Kraftwerk album and he had this ruthless, European, electro, pop sound going through his being and because of what he was DJing, he just naturally sculpted it and featured all the elements that enhanced that vision.

***

'Violator' was a real blossoming success for Mute. It was double the sales from the previous album, so that's obviously wonderful.

But beyond that, the way that they nailed the electronic sound, the kind of continuity that I see with the German electropop, was always very important to the band in the 1980s, when I first met them.

And also very important to Daniel and very inspirational, which is one of the reasons that we were all so delighted with the big success in Germany, initially, before wider success in Europe and America, because, actually, we were such huge fans of German electronic music and Krautrock.

This blend of Krautrock and electronic music that we all loved coming out of Germany, which the Germans didn't even seem to appreciate!

I think it's a real endorsement of their electronic music tradition that the record was so successful. That would have been nice, to have a huge success like that, with a record that is so in the tradition, for me, of German electronic pop music.

Maybe their fan base is open to change. Because there is a big change from 'Speak & Spell' to 'Black Celebration'. They always seemed to be trying to do something different

It's different when you look back though. That's a different way of discovering music. Because I am a fan of a lot of music that I didn't grow up with, often as I wasn't around at the time.

But I go back and discover the music and think, "Oh, this is fantastic!" I think you have a broader view, I don't know why that is.

Perhaps that's why they have kept the dedicated fans, it's because people don't want endless repeats of the same stuff. Like, do we want 'Iron Man 12'?

They are very creative people and I think it is very challenging for a creative person to do the same again, to say, "Okay, we will just knock out another one!".

It's not easy but certain kinds of people can do it. Like authors writing a whole series of novels. Certain kinds of writers might be able to do that.

But I'm not sure that the members of Depeche have those skills, which is a good thing.

That's the core within many fans, too. When a huge record like 'Violator' comes along, then a whole wealth of new fans get picked up. They might not stay on the journey because then, three records later, when they are doing something very different like 'Exciter', the fans who came in only at 'Violator' may have already gone off somewhere else and found something else. But many others remain.

Neil Ferris (UK), plugger for Mute Records

Violator was a turning point if you like. It was an album that excited a huge amount of people.

My involvement with Depeche was radio and TV. So from day one, it was a constant battle for me because the media were not hugely supportive of DM.

But as they grew, especially in America and in Germany, it was a different kettle of fish because people looked at them as a huge rock band. In England, we were always dealing with the fact that people thought of DM as the band that made the 'Speak & Spell' album.

So to get people to embrace DM was very difficult and, for me, what was even more difficult was that were my favourite band of all time!

Not only was there a very, very close relationship between Daniel Miller and myself, because I was involved from the start, but it was just trying to get people in the media to understand just how much I believed in it, and that was very, very difficult.

Having said that 'Violator' was a turning point, 'Music For The Masses' was also a turning point, of sorts, so it was kind of like we were growing all the time. And it's kind of difficult to pick out one album and say, "that was a massive change," because I think we were growing from the very start.

I was very close to Daniel and obviously close to the band but essentially what would happen is that I wouldn't hear any music until Daniel was in a position where he wanted me to hear it. I probably was the person that heard the recordings before anyone else but I didn't hear anything until Daniel was really confident because he liked to play it to me and watch my face.

I think it would have been 'Personal Jesus' or 'Enjoy The Silence' that I heard first. It was very, very different.

Daniel always chose the singles. Funnily enough, what would happen, he would play me the record, he would then say to me, "Take it home and play it to Gill," my wife, who was also in the record industry.

And we'd go through a little scenario when that would happen on every record where Daniel would ring later and say, "Well, what do you think? No actually, what does Gill think?"

I knew 'Personal Jesus' was going to be a huge record but I also knew I was going to have problems with it on the radio because of the content.

I remember at the time [BBC Radio One presenter] Simon Mayo, who was doing the breakfast show, was incredibly religious and said to me, "What's the song about?" I seem to remember telling him that the song was about everybody needing to have something in their lives that they could look up to and so everyone had to have their own personal Jesus, so that's what the song is about.

Of course, that's not what the song's about at all – but that helped us get Record Of The Week.

When you look at the video, it's obvious that the song's not quite that. But then the video is always someone else's interpretation, so I've always believed and said you make a video as an artist and it's all about making it exactly as you hear it, the way you feel it, the way you want it.

But then you hand that track over to someone else who then has a view and a vision and creates a three-minute film that is not actually yours, it's theirs.

Daniel would approach me and say, "Look, this is what we're going to do."

But I would then make comments about which mix I thought was right for radio or television, and whether the length was right.

I tend to think you have to have gems on albums. I think back to the day when people were just buying albums as a body of work. I think there needed to be things on the album that potentially were not something that you'd choose as a single but may even be a stronger track or the better track, but maybe not right as a single.

If you look at my iPhone, for when I go out running, 'Halo' is still on there – even all these years later.

I'm sure I'd have sat down with the band and just said, "It is great," or, "Love the album," or "I think it is brilliant." And I'm sure they'd have made the usual comment, "Well, it's all down to you now – you'd better get out there and do it."

I only represented things that I really, really believed in and so the only clients I had were people I was passionate about.

Therefore the whole essence of representing DM or representing the Human League or Heaven 17 or Japan or Spandau Ballet, or any of the bands I represented, was because I absolutely loved them and it didn't matter what money was on the table.

I remember turning down Peter Gabriel because I said, "Look, I'm not going to work with Peter Gabriel because he's not my thing, he's established and every band I've got, I broke."

So, therefore, with DM I was going out because I believed so much in the band, it was very personal.

The people in the media, who I was going to talk to, knew that it was always really personal. So when I went and talked to people about DM or any of the bands I represented, you were talking about my personal taste.

There's no question that early on we had to prostitute them to do a lot of TV and stuff that we wouldn't have done at a different age.

In those days you had to do Saturday morning kids' TV, you had to do 'Jim'll Fix It', you had to do all that kind of stuff. Where I really wanted DM was on 'Whistle Test' and eventually we did do it and we did do 'The Tube', things like that.

If you were talking now, you'd be saying, "Actually, we're gonna do no TV apart from 'Later With Jools Holland' and you might do a Jonathan Ross interview with a performance."

Depeche, therefore, was very much about having done all of the pop shows, Razzamataz and all that stuff because we had to get them broken, we had to establish them, we had to get out there.

Back in those days, the only television you did back in those days was kids' TV, so if you were trying to break music, pre-MTV, it was all about, how do you get this band broken?

The only way to do it is to have the record on BBC Radio 1, because there was only Radio 1.

It changed with 'Black Celebration' and you have to say Anton did give it that kind of grainy, very cool look – a darker look.

And that doesn't mean to say that the band weren't becoming darker and cooler – they were, there was no question. And also obviously through this period, it was true to say that there were other influences on the band which, to a large extent, were Alan. So, I think his influences were getting stronger and stronger as we were going along.

Obviously, Flood is a genius but do not underestimate what Daniel brings to every record as well.

We all believed so passionately in DM and this was the new record, which was a staggering piece of work, so we knew we had a massive record on our hands.

The key was what order do we release the tracks? You listen to 'Violator' and you say, "This is incredible. This is rammed full of big tracks."

But what do you do? I mean, 'Waiting For The Night' is such a great song. 'Halo' is phenomenal.

I remember saying to Daniel, "God, 'Halo' should be a single!" But Daniel was saying, "No, no, no!"

To be fair, if you look at that album, 'Policy Of Truth' is such a big track, and so is 'Enjoy The Silence'. You could even say 'Clean' could potentially be a single.

I think the band were very positive. I think things were starting to happen globally and I think we'd turned a corner. Everyone was feeling very comfortable and I do remember Daniel with a big grin on his face when he played 'Violator' – he was very proud of it.

I always think with DM that one of the problems is that, other than the fans, people don't realise what an amazing record it is until way after the event. I think that's always been true of DM records.

The fans, obviously, will have got 'Violator', will have loved it when it came out, and just thought it was the greatest record that they've made to that point.

I think 'Violator' is such an amazing record and that's its legacy. It's an amazingly well-made record, with great songs and confidence about it that I don't think we had before 'Violator'.

I don't think the band had changed at all at that stage. As one of the few artists I worked with, I don't think the fame and all of that changed them, apart from that it became more of a machine. The pressure was getting bigger and bigger, but they were still these four guys from Basildon.

Stephane Devillers (Belgium), fan

I've been a fan since 1985, when a friend of mine played 'Shake The Disease' to me, and then 'Master And Servant', a live version from Basel in 1984.

I was really astonished by what I heard and what appealed to me was how original the sounds were.

Depeche Mode used sounds that had never been heard before, and it was therefore really exciting.

After that, I decided to get all the releases that I could.

At that time, there was obviously no internet and I lived in a small town. I would have to take a 25-minute train ride to Brussels, then I would go to several record shops, get the train back and finally, get to put on the vinyl or CDs, and press play. It was such an exciting way of getting hold of new music - no YouTube, no iTunes, no Amazon!

We all have our favourite Depeche album. Mine is 'Music For The Masses' because that's the band at their best.

Since 'Speak & Spell', all their albums have improved, evolving from teen pop to industrial and finally perfect electropop. 'Strangelove' is the perfect example of what DM are all about: catchy tunes, Dave Gahan's unique voice and, most importantly, a great melody.

I remember when I first heard 'Personal Jesus'. At the time I was collecting bootleg live tapes and I had a lot of penpals all around the world.

In mid-1989, a pen pal from the UK sent me a tape. He'd recorded 'Personal Jesus' from a telephone line. The band had put an ad in a newspaper with just the words "Your Own Personal Jesus", and a telephone number.

You called and heard the recording! I could barely hear the guitar riff and Dave's voice, but I was so excited!

The fact that they'd used guitars wasn't a surprise. They had started using them on previous songs like 'Strangelove', 'Pleasure Little Treasure' and 'Route 66'. Even if the guitar riff was bluesy, the song was still electronic; it wasn't a 180-degree change.

I loved the single and 12-inch versions. François Kevorkian produced some fantastic remixes.

At the end of the year, Depeche appeared on 'Peter's Pop-Show', a German TV show where all the artists performed two songs.

As I watched the show, I wondered what DM would perform as the second track? 'Never Let Me Down Again'? 'Everything Counts'?

Then they started playing a completely new song: 'Enjoy The Silence'.

I have to confess that I didn't like it at first. The beat sounded too techno, the guitar riff sounded like a Cure B-side and the whole song sounded too commercial.

That was a real turning point I thought. But after a few listens, I got used to it and understood that what would follow would be in the same vein.

The video was beautiful and weird at the same time – Anton Corbijn's usual touch – and MTV put it on heavy rotation. You could watch it almost every hour!

Given how great the two singles released before the album were, expectations for 'Violator' were high!

When I got my hands on the CD, the first shock was the sleeve! The contrast between the title and the rose was so strong.

That's another trademark of the band: choosing weird album names.

The first listen was confirmation of what I had expected: the band had a new and up-to-date sound. They were using sounds resulting from messing about with machines, guitars and real drums.

While 'Black Celebration' and 'Music For The Masses' are almost concept albums that you can listen to in their entirety, 'Violator' sounds more like a hits compilation.

'World In My Eyes', 'Personal Jesus', 'Enjoy The Silence', 'Policy Of Truth' plus 'Halo' (which could have been a fifth single), along with great album tracks like 'Waiting For The Night' or 'Clean', plus the usual Martin songs. What else could you ask for?

What made 'Violator' such a great album is the team that worked on it. Flood and Alan Wilder were the perfect duo to work on Martin Gore's demos.

I knew that they had really made it when my school friends started asking me to give them a copy of 'Violator'.

Until then, I was the only one listening to this weird band – the one with a guy who wore skirts – and then, all of a sudden, I was the guy who was a fan of that great band, you know the one with the singer with his crown, who sings 'Enjoy The Silence'.

The album received some of the best reviews the band has ever had from the press and some of their detractors started to recognise their talent, at last. And the fact that they won a Brit Award for Best Single for 'Enjoy The Silence' was really the icing on the cake.

When the 'World Violation Tour' started in the US, I remember being very jealous of the Americans. They always started their tours in Europe and they had ended the 'Music For The Masses' tour in America.

I had the feeling that they wanted to continue their breakthrough in the US and that was a good move for their career.

My first tour date was, obviously, Brussels and it was the date in Europe.

Dave once said that American audiences are great at making a big noise but Europeans sing along more. When he started to sing the first line of the concert opening track 'World In My Eyes', with more than 8,000 fans joining in, you could see the smile on his face.

I saw four shows during that tour: Brussels, Paris (the second night), Lievin and finally, Strasbourg.

The Paris Bercy gig was a particularly great show, not least because there is something special between the Parisian audience and the band.

Bercy is such a great venue – not too big and with a great sound. And the setlist was almost perfect.

While playing most of the 'Violator' album, they played old favourites such as 'Master And Servant', 'Shake The Disease', and even 'Everything Counts' in a great remixed version.

Martin also performed two acoustic songs, which was a nice surprise!

For the first time, they also added two giant screens to their stage set, featuring special films and clips made by Corbijn, which gave a really great new dimension to the shows.

It was a very unusual thing to do at the time, although now everyone does it.

Strangely, no live album or video from the tour was ever released, probably because '101' had recently been released. This gives it a special, almost mythical status in that it's something that fans keep hoping will eventually happen.

The end of the tour was like a hangover. I had the feeling that, with this successful album and tour, they had reached the top and wondered what the future would be. I also felt really proud.

'My' band had made it, critics had finally come round and 'Violator' was going to be a cult album.

Chapter 6

Advertising That Money Can't Buy

'Depeche fans are affable, a happy group of people... yet suddenly it was a mob! But, you know, it was really just people trying to get to the band."

***

Los Angeles, March 1990. California's largest city again features strongly in the Depeche Mode story.

After the first two singles from 'Violator' – 'Personal Jesus' and 'Enjoy The Silence' – had successfully managed to whip fans into a frenzy, and also stir the often cynical loins of critics, attention turned to how the band might capitalise on an increasing sense of anticipation and excitement ahead of the release of 'Violator'.

In almost every country where Depeche had a significant fan base, and by 1990 this figure would easily have been pushing into the dozens, preparing for the release of a new album would follow a familiar pattern for the band.

A single or two, as was the case with 'Violator', would have preceded the launch of the album, often with the first song hitting the airwaves as far as six to eight months before the album was released.

Each single would have its associated radio and TV play, with the latter more often than not featuring an accompanying lip-synced performance to a backing track.

Interestingly, despite their respective high chart positions (13 and six), neither the release of 'Personal Jesus' or 'Enjoy

The Silence' led to an appearance by the band on their home turf's high-profile weekly music TV show, 'Top Of The Pops'.

Still, such appearances would be planned weeks in advance and would often mean the band and their entourage would head off to a European city somewhere to perform the song and cram in countless numbers of interviews with local media.

The merry-go-round of PAs (personal appearances) and interviews ensured the band were front and centre in as many markets and channels as possible during the critical single-buying period.

Innumerable features would appear in the niche music newspapers (such as the 'NME' in the UK), plus many of the mainstream music and entertainment magazines were on-board by then, such as 'Rolling Stone' and 'Q'.

Despite their general apathy towards parts of the media, especially in the UK where the music press had often been far from kind in its coverage of the band, Depeche had a system that was exhausting, yet successful.

The band would rarely conduct interviews as a four-piece, primarily to save time rather than (at this stage) because they'd fallen out with one another.

Dave Gahan and Alan Wilder or Martin Gore and Andy Fletcher, for example, would do the rounds of the radio and TV stations, magazines and newspapers to espouse the virtues of their latest public output.

And then they would move on to the next city and the process would start again.

In 1990 however, the American marketplace for promoting and selling records was one where it was generally still extremely difficult to do so efficiently and effectively.

Until 'Violator', much of Depeche's exposure to US audiences had come from its commitment to playing shows across the country and plugging those appearances close to the date of each performance.

They were, in many respects, still seen as an underground band in the eyes of those in the mainstream music industry when it came to an album launch, relying on radio play from local or university radio stations.

The 'Music For The Masses Tour' triggered the beginnings of a rethink as to how Depeche would have to tackle the US from a promotional perspective for albums in the future.

The band had played some 40 shows in North America over two legs in late-1987 and mid-1988, culminating in the 101st show at the Pasadena Rose Bowl in June, but also taking in destinations as diverse as Austin in Texas, Salt Lake City in Utah and Iowa's Cedar Rapids.

The touring and media schedule had worked, pushing the band towards the edges of its then-still cult status, as many of those in the mainstream media woke up and realised that another group of four young lads from Britain were causing a hell of a stir on college campuses.

The triumph of the Rose Bowl gig and the fever surrounding the release of the subsequent '101' movie and live record had shown that not only was there an enormous fan base in the US but it was one that could help propel Depeche even further into the consciousness of the country's mainstream record-buying public.

But in many respects, Depeche were in unchartered territory, as was its UK label Mute Records.

The buzz amongst fans following the releases of 'Personal Jesus' and 'Enjoy The Silence', coupled with a confidence in the Depeche camp knowing that the 'Violator' album was clearly a massive step up in its creative output, showed there was the potential for something big – bigger than Pasadena and '101'-- to happen in the history of the band.

Touring relentlessly for years and working the local radio circuit in the US is one thing; how to launch an album on the national stage, in a country as diverse and big as America, is another matter entirely.

The band's US label Sire came up with a plan. They and Mute joined up with the Los Angeles radio station K-ROQ, long-time Depeche Mode supporters, and announced a 'Violator' signing session at the record shop The Wherehouse which was based at 3rd and La Cienega in Los Angeles.

Prior to the signing, Martin was interviewed by telephone on the show Request Video. The host Jim 'The Poorman' Trenton asked Goreif he was aware that it had been predicted that a crowd of ten thousand people would attend the event.

Gore replied, saying, "I think everybody is getting too hyped up about it. It's going to be really disappointing." Events proved Martin wrong by quite a distance.

The event was scheduled to take place on 20 March 1990 and was due to start around 9pm. The demand for anything Depeche Mode related was so high that fans began camping out the night before the event and by 8pm on March 20, there were indeed around 10,000 fans queuing at the store as had been predicted. That number would only increase as the start time approached.

It is worth noting that by this time in their career, Depeche Mode were an established band, all aged in their late twenties or early thirties. They were not a British invasion era Beatles causing a teen frenzy, nor were they at the stage in their career Duran Duran found themselves when they first went to America and were besieged by the teen hordes.

Depeche Mode's audience had grown up with the band and could be considered to be more mature than the armies of teenagers who were best known for following around various bands in a state of frenzy. The type of audience Depeche Mode had made the events that unfolded at The Wherehouse all the more remarkable.

Here was a band who were still far from critically acclaimed at home and who had become huge in America with little if any mainstream support. Despite these things, people were camping out overnight just to get an autograph and thousands, yes thousands, more people joined those campers the next day in the hope of meeting their heroes

It seems almost impossible to believe and, had the event not received widespread coverage after its conclusion, would anyone really accept that Depeche Mode had created such a frenzy that their fans went on the rampage?

The event was broadcast live on KROQ with Richard Blade interviewing the band before the doors opened at 9pm. It was already obvious that the size of the crowd outside the store had far exceeded all expectations. Gahan told Richard that he was "very moved" by the sheer volume of fans at The Wherehouse adding that he hadn't expected many people to turn up at all.

Jim Trenton was present too with a 'Request Video' camera crew and their footage shows just how frantic events became as the evening proceeded. Jim manages to interview the band too with Gahan telling him that it was "really flattering" that so many people had come to see Depeche Mode. He added that he'd heard that around 17,000 people were there.

The doors opened at 9pm and fans started filing in, offering anything Depeche Mode related to the band for them to sign. As well as sundry 'Violator' related items, footage of the event shows a diverse range of Depeche Mode items including the band's least-loved single 'It's Called A Heart'. Ever the professionals, they even signed that.

It quickly became apparent that things were starting to go wrong outside The Wherehouse. Fans were being crushed against the store's windows and there were growing concerns for everyone's safety. KROQ was broadcasting live throughout the event and they started passing on police warnings to their listeners.

Blade first announced that he had heard from the police that fans were to "keep it mellow or the cops will close it down." He later advised listeners that "things are pretty serious" and he sounds genuinely worried on the broadcast.

Only one hour into the three-hour event, Depeche Mode were forced to leave the building due to Police safety concerns. Blade announced the end of the event, warning fans that he had been told that "If people do not leave, they are going to jail." Depeche Mode were smuggled out of the store into waiting limousines and they left.

That was not the end of it, however.

Fans reacted badly to the news that their heroes were not going to be signing autographs for them. Those near the store started banging on its windows. Others, mainly drunken fans, it must be said, started throwing missiles and others jumped on cars and news vans. Police lined the streets flanked by mounted officers on horseback while police helicopters monitored events from the air. It is safe to say that nobody expected any of this.

Local news channels quickly started reporting what was going on, with each broadcast seeming to report the presence of increasing numbers of fans. Quite quickly, the event became described as a riot. All that did was increase the volume of news coverage and the next morning, Depeche Mode's riot was the main story on the many news channels in the LA area.

At this point, everything just got a bit silly. Local councilman Zev Yaroslavsky acted as you would expect any politician would do and quickly jumped upon a bandwagon of his own making, claiming that KROQ-FM and The Wherehouse should cover the costs incurred in policing the event. Other talking heads on the news expressed their disgust with the fans' behaviour.

Suddenly, promoting Depeche Mode in the US was no longer a struggle. They were the band everyone was talking about. They were the band that caused a riot.

To apologise to fans, and perhaps fearing that litigation may follow, Daniel Miller ordered the production of a cassette to give to fans inconvenienced by the incident.

The cassette, which features a selection of Depeche Mode interviews and the Metal Mix of 'Some Great Reward' track 'Something To Do', a mix previously unavailable in the US, could be obtained directly from KROQ by writing into the station. There were 25,000 copies of the cassette produced and it remains collectable to this day.

It is of course entirely correct to say that damage was caused to public and private property because of the event and seven people did suffer minor injuries. Whether this was a riot however is a matter of debate but the more people referred to the riot, the better that was for promotion.

The band were asked about it at a pre-'World Violation Tour' press conference. Wilder said, "It's not what I would call a riot." Prompted by Gahan, he went on to say, "Chelsea on a Saturday afternoon – that's a riot," referring to Fletch's favourite football team and their then notoriously troublesome fans. Unlike the publicity-hungry Yaroslavsky, the band saw the humour in The Wherehouse incident.

While there is no question at all of The Wherehouse disturbance being planned by the band, the label or KROQ, 'Violator' and its forthcoming tour could not have asked for any better publicity.

Everybody knew who Depeche Mode were and the event was reported in the music press around the world. Anticipation for the album and tour could not get any higher – and all it took was one small riot.

Bruce Kirkland (USA), marketing and publicity for Depeche Mode

'Violator' was sort of the apex of their career because they had worked their way up through the food chain, primarily through building an audience, and that record was the pinnacle of it.

The stars line up like that very seldom in the career of a band and yet we knew that when we first heard the demos.

We just knew that it was a special record.

If you talk to artists or musicians, they look like they have some massive strategic plan but often they do not.

I remember when I was working at Capitol, sitting with The Beatles and Neal Aspinal. I would come up with all these strategic plans for this and that and 'The Anthology' and stuff and he'd say, "Bruce, you are missing the point!" Nothing was planned, it all just happened

And to a certain extent, that's exactly how worked with Depeche. With respect to '101', I mean, the band were incredibly popular in LA, they couldn't have done the Rose Bowl event anywhere else in the world.

Because KROQ pretty much supported the band, they were extraordinarily popular in this market and they were building in other markets. The mathematics of '101' and the Rose Bowl show were that we could probably do three, four maybe even five LA Forum gigs, which was the arena, so the numbers instead were saying, "Let's play the Rose Bowl!" because of the impact it would create.

Nobody would expect a band of that level to play a stadium at that point. No one was doing it. So we did it, filmed it. That to me was one of the biggest marketing achievements we had because it was creating a perception of largesse and that bit wasn't an accident.

We were very deliberate about that because at the point the band had made the transition from a pop band in England then Vince left and then they were trying to be a credible band in the European markets and really on fire to be able to export the picture 65,000 people at the Rose Bowl back into Europe people going, "Oh my god, they are huge in America!"

They were huge in one market in America. They were still selling out arenas but it was one night and Radio City Music Hall, but this was a phenomenon. This was an aberration.

So you felt that coming out of it, that momentum, you knew you were on a roll at that point because you were starting to expand the base but we were doing it by our rules, not selling out, and that was very important to the band.

So now, if 'Violator' hadn't come along and delivered everything on the expectation that this thing was moving at a rapid rate, then it probably would have folded, but the right record came at the right time. The groundswell was right there, it was all set up.

Daniel and the band were precious about music getting out, so I'm sitting here in America but you know we heard tracks at that early point.

'Personal Jesus' wasn't my favourite song, frankly. Three or four songs came over and those were sort of the planned hits. We just knew something big was happening.

Okay, so it was a big decision to go with Flood because at that point they'd used Daniel up until 'Black Celebration' and then Dave Bascombe for 'Music For The Masses'. He had this idea of a synthpop band but using slightly more natural instruments and he saw Depeche as being the right sort of band between the two.

I heard 'Violator' as a step forward from 'Music For The Masses'. I didn't hear it as a diametrically different position. But I think the songwriting was exceptional

When these things happen it's magic. They could have gone off the rails after the Rose Bowl. But it was just the right album at the right time. There was this guy, Eddie Rosenblatt, who was at David Geffen records and he was always asked about Nirvana and what the label's role was in breaking 'Nevermind' and he said, "We got out of the way!"

So there was a certain sense around 'Violator' that you really couldn't fuck it up because the work had been done before and the support from the band's fans and the growing fan base was just ready to take off.

Still, I have no doubt that they wrote 'Violator' for themselves. They were obviously tuned in to what was going on business-wise but their motivations were totally different in those days. There was creative motivation, not financial, for sure.

'Personal Jesus', as the first single, was that sort of divergent move away from the band's sound.

There was no management per se. It was just the band. They would make the decisions and ask, "What do you think?"

I think in retrospect it was instrumental in bringing another audience and a buzz to the band because there was a rootsy American feel to it.

'Enjoy The Silence' was an obvious first single for me, but because of where the band was in terms of the fanbase and their expectations, 'Personal Jesus' just warmed the market up even more.

In those days, alternative radio was a powerhouse and they were really working your first single way out in front of the album for you and you were dropping the second around the time of the album.

***

We were like a marketing company. We would set up and coordinate everything for them in the US on behalf of the band, working with the record label.

But there was a major divergence of opinion about that second single because, from the label's point of view, which was Warner Brothers, you knew they liked 'Personal Jesus' because of its rootsy thing.

So we had a massive argument with the label about the second single. In those days you would call it a 'setup track' before the album, which would be your big radio hit around the time of the album for maximum PR exposure.

So we had a big argument about it – 'Enjoy The Silence' versus 'World In My Eyes'. There was a big lobby at Warner Brothers!

In fact, even 'Policy Of Truth' was more uptempo, rockier, and perhaps a logical follow-up to 'Personal Jesus'.

I remember we were having meetings at Warner Brothers and it got pretty hostile. Those that run the company had to come in and mediate you know, cause it got pretty fierce.

Daniel was very much on the side of 'Enjoy The Silence' – "This is the song!" he said. He was looking at it from England and the world as a whole, and I'm looking at it from the US.

But there was this kind of another point of view because The Cure came out with 'Lovesong' – a big top 40 hit – and then the album 'Disintegration'.

So those two things happened simultaneously and you can't overlook that in terms of overall strategy because this is the same audience you are talking to – it's that alternative audience and they were becoming much more mainstream in America.

'Enjoy The Silence' had the potential and so we knew there were two big bands at that time, Depeche and The Cure.

Anyway, 'Policy Of Truth' came next but I still thought 'World In My Eyes' was a much bigger track. I still think that track had the ability to take the album from 2.8 million to 7.5 million in the US.

It had a massive groove. It was a sexy song.

***

Fletch was really the go-to guy from my point of view and I'd talk to him sometimes two or three times a day.

At that time the industry was changing and the retail deals you could cut could jet your records up the charts. They were smart enough to know what was going on. It was just a much more healthy environment and transparent. I still use it to this day if people are trying to figure out how to exist in the current industry. Depeche were the model.

At the time, they were still an alternative band in the eyes of a lot of people. We had a lot more attention from the label because of the residuals but the jury was out still because in those days everything was dictated by airplay, so there was no guarantee. In fact, I would have conversations with the band where they would be like, "Please don't put us on top 40 radio again because we'll lose our credibility!"

That was a big part of my job – maintaining credibility and being commercially successful.

I got to know the band and understand the marketplace and the sensibility of the product we were dealing with. That's where the skillset comes in. Everyone thinks it just happens and for most bands, it sort of does.

But there's a lot more in this case, with a band whose primary strength was their live work, to the extent that because you have a live audience it means that you don't have to follow the dictates of the industry as you have a lot of independence.

Here's a band that has built its base from the ground up, so it's paramount that you don't blow the audience because you've lost that control. We could say to the record company we are not doing something and they would say, "What do you mean you are not doing that?". We would say: "Well, it doesn't work with our model. We are here, we are playing to our fans and that's our bread and butter!"

So if there was anything the record company wanted to do that we felt would harm that relationship with the fan base, we wouldn't do it and we'd just be able to say that.

I think at that point the band were all pretty much strapped in for the ride because they were touring and they were always really relaxed about everything.

I'd go over to Europe while they were on tour, for two or three days, and take them through what was going on and they'd be cool! There was never really any real dissension. This was a great time for the band – money wasn't really a motivation and they weren't four business guys, like investment bankers, all sitting down trying to figure out how to sort of turn $3 million into $50 million.

***

I don't think I can take the credit for The Wherehouse. But maybe I was an architect of it...

We knew that the groundswell for 'Personal Jesus' had already been blowing up and we knew that all of that momentum from Rose Bowl and '101' was there.

KROQ were really instrumental, so if anyone can take credit then they could, as Depeche Mode were like a franchise band for them. It was almost as if they would give their entire annual marketing budget to Depeche to make a record because it would do more for them as a radio station and their ratings than all the billboards in LA could ever deliver. Depeche Mode was the sound of the station.

So I was talking to them a lot and I said that we were looking to do an 'in-store', because we were looking for a big launch event in LA. There wasn't really anything you could do in any other market other than LA, so we talked about it.

We thought we would do it more of an unannounced thing. The record company really wasn't sort of tracking what we were up to, and the radio station knew it was potentially a volatile situation. So I said, "Ok, let's do it two days before." I was pushing to get more but if you'd do this on the radio for a week it would have been mayhem so we compromised on two to three days to announce it.

The boys are up for it, come to The Wherehouse and they'll be signing albums! But I knew what was going to happen because the fanbase was fanatical at that point and that's why KROQ was trying to dampen it down a little bit before.

But I think in retrospect there were a lot of issues on the night. It was scary.

Our biggest issue was logistics, getting everyone through the line and signatures. At one point the police were there, the fire department, the whole thing. It was news all over America!

We were communicating with the police and fire department and they were all saying, "Yeah, shut it down!"

People were hearing it on the radio and coming down to make it worse, but it became the indelible image: the frogmarching jackboots, the riot police marching down, it was incredibly scary.

I think everyone was tense and you don't know what a mob crowd can do. Depeche fans were an affable, happy group of people and suddenly, it was a mob. But it was just people trying to get to the band that's all it was.

They had us there for a couple of hours and then we were just trying to push people through because the agitation was coming from people who knew we were only going to be there for a certain amount of time. I guess many were thinking, "Oh, I'm not going to get in so I'll cut the line!"

The Wherehouse had done these before. They were up for it and they did these on a regular basis and could handle events like that. But nothing like this. At the end of the day, it was a big deal.

No one got hurt but it was on all the news. If you look at all the news reports, you have all these harebrained anchors banging on about Depeche Mode. The band wasn't a phenomenon in the mainstream media so for them this was an aberration. "Who are these people?!?'

And this was on the eve of the album coming out. Remarkable timing!

But you don't even know when these things are going to happen. I thought that maybe we'll get maybe 3,000 or 4,000 people – that was the expectation, not that they'd close La Cienega Boulevard!

Not to be sort of blase about it as a marketing person, but this is what you look for – you are wanting a national event, and it was an international one eventually.

This was actually the sensibility behind doing the Rose Bowl, '101' phenomenon and filming it.

It was always like we are doing this stuff, you don't recognise it in Europe and this is what's going here. I learned a lot, like the band, but realised they do not like interviews.

With the Rose Bowl, for example, I was really pushing hard to get an Arts or Leisure-type cover, like on a Sunday in the 'Los Angeles Times'. Getting that was a big deal, so I promised the band that we'd get the cover and it was, well, they are not going to talk!

The 'LA Times', to their credit, said, "Well, what's the big deal about these guys?" So they said if the band won't talk to them, then they'd go to talk to their fans. They did the cover story because the band were big enough to warrant it. Readers were going to understand the band through their fans. You got a 16-year-old girl in Orange County talking about alienation and depression and relating entirely to Martin's lyrics and then we thought, "Oh, wow, this is why this is happening!"

***

Dodger Stadium in 1990 was another big moment. Sold it out in a day! We did Giants Stadium, in New York, too. And that was all because of that little radio station, WDRE.

The relationship between media and audience is just a phenomenal thing but that was a big one again.

These guys were complete professionals and they liked the road. Every night and it never changed.

When I first started working with them, every night as soon as the show was out, J. D. Fanger would be up there with the audience and they'd bring fans back and get the old jukebox and they'd meet and talk with their fans.

If you'd done two nights at Dodger Stadium, with any band, it would be like Coachella headliners – it's like royalty. You can't get near them, with this and that protocol.

There was more hoi polloi around support act Electronic. The Electronic compound was like some kind of incredible event going on, then you'd go over to Depeche, who were the headliners, and it was just hanging around and no protocol – just the easiest, most relaxed environment, with no pretentiousness.

I think The Cure's 'Disintegration' is a classic. Peter Gabriel's 'Soul' is a classic.. Pink Floyd's 'Dark Side Of The Moon' is a classic. 'Violator is a classic'.

These albums transcend generations and they are reinventing their audience all the time.

Anecdotally, being at LiveAid in London and watching The Who – it's 250 000 people at Hyde Park looking at them as if they are at a museum or something. They are good, yeah, look at that, he smashes his guitar!

But when Pink Floyd came on it the whole crowd elevated because everyone in that audience was listening to that record. It wasn't like some sort of relic from the past – it was as important to them as when it first came out.

'Violator' has that same vibe – it's timeless.

Andy Franks (UK), production director for the 'World Violation Tour'

I remember The Wherehouse incident because I was heavily involved in it as well.

I went to have a meeting with the Los Angeles Chief of Police when we were first having a discussion about doing the signing there.

I was saying to him, "Right, the first thing I want to say is that these guys are quite popular and we are expecting to get quite a few people, you know. They are a big underground band!"

This guy was so sort of blase about the whole thing and he said, "Look, sonny, we do these sorts of things all the time, we know how it all works, you don't need to tell us... This is the LAPD, we are used to controlling violence and this is what we do!"

I went up to him after the event, when he came back to our hotel to apologise. The guy was a broken man, he could hardly speak, he was so hoarse!

And he was saying, "I gotta say, you guys were absolutely fucking right - you know I've never seen anything like this in my life!"

Anyway, LA-based Radio station KROQ had played and been a big supporter of the band, so it was sort of involved and had been building it up quite a lot.

We went that day to have lunch with some Warner Brothers executives and quite a few other people.

On the way back, we got the limo drivers to swing by The Wherehouse so we could have a look. KROQ presenter

Richard Blade was saying on air, "We've got two blocks of people and now we are up to five blocks and now we've got eight blocks and we are up to ten blocks."

And we so thought, "Oh fucking hell, here he goes again!" – always the mad overstating and overthinking. When we were about 14-15 blocks away, suddenly we saw people that sort of looked like they were in a bit of a line and we thought, "Oh, this is a bit weird."

Then we started to realise that it was a line of people and then, of course, somebody spotted the band and word got out. The band had also thought that they were turning up for a record-signing and for just 15 minutes but when we told them they were going to be there for about three hours they were pretty miffed about it.

They were saying, "Are you kidding? Three hours, we are not signing records for three hours!"

When we got into the place, because of the logistics of how it was, we had to drive straight into the car park at the record store and walk in through the side. They'd done a great job of keeping everybody in line but of course, once the band was there people were saying, "Fuck it, we're breaking line!" and the whole place was surrounded.

It became really scary because we were inside this building that was pretty much on its own - we were sort of in a sea of people. You could see them leaning off the side of the building and looking in the windows of the record store.

I remember it was sort of like plate glass, so it was about three or four inches thick and it was bending with this force of people trying to push in to see the band.

It was a very scary moment. They got on with some sort of signing but it just became very apparent that there was no way that they were going to sign or be able to sign for the people that were there but also because of the number of people building up outside.

And, by now, the police were getting involved and there were mounted officers and everything, so we had to find a way to sneak them out.

But no, if we are going to get them out they've got to go out in front of the building so that everyone could see they are leaving otherwise they'll never believe it.

We managed to turn the cars around and get them into the vehicles and rush them out. The band were, of course, absolutely delighted about the whole thing but even happier that we managed to get them back into the hotel in about two-and-a-half hours from arriving at the place.

And then, putting on the TV and the police have blocked off the road because now people are crowding around and it was all over the news at the time – breaking news!

"British Rock band Depeche Mode are causing quite a stir. There are 15,000 people here!!"

A DJ on UK station Radio 1 at the time, Simon Mayo, thought it was a big sort of set-up and said that they made up that there were 15,000 people outside and, well, made quite a lot of fun of the whole thing.

We sent him news footage of the thing and he made a public apology on the radio that he'd made a mistake.

It couldn't have been better timing. I think they ended up having to pay like $25 000 to the city of Los Angeles for cleaning up. There was a lot of police there in the end! It was like a mini-war zone. It was incredible.

In your wildest dreams, you couldn't plan a thing like that – it just wouldn't have worked and again it was a testament to the strength of the fans of Depeche, which nobody else gave a shit about or thought anything of – but they all turned up!

Rob Rohm (USA), fan and member of the crowd at The Wherehouse

I first saw Depeche Mode in concert in 1986 on the 'Black Celebration' tour in Los Angeles. I saw them on back-to-back nights at Irvine Meadows, closer to where I lived in Orange County.

A few years later I was in the front row at the Rose Bowl in Pasadena.

I was a 19-year-old at the time in 1990 and went very early during the day to secure a place in line with two girl friends.

It was surprising how long the lines were already. This was the first time I had ever attended any type of autograph signing event.

Although the lines already seemed extremely long, especially considering our arrival early in the day, we still thought that we'd be able to get the band's autographs.

In hindsight, the event was extremely disorganised from early on. There really should have been some type of system in place to cut off the line at a certain point.

I brought a painting with me (that I still have) that I did, based on the image Anton Corbijn shot for the back of the 'Personal Jesus' 12-inch single.

It shows a naked woman with her hand on the wall standing in front of Dave Gahan with his hands on her shoulders.

The painting is 20 inches by 20 inches and was unframed at the time. That was what I intended to have signed by the band.

I had also been inspired by the band to write and record music, so I also brought some demo tapes with me. There is a clip of me on the evening news where my painting is visible above my head – I was trying to keep it from getting damaged in the chaos.

As we were waiting for the night to fall, the line grew larger and larger.

Finally, Depeche Mode arrived and excitement was in the air. At some point after little movement of the line, I think people grew more anxious.

Word was travelling through the line that we probably weren't going to get in and they were going to shut it down.

The realisation that the band may not be able to sign autographs for everyone in line definitely had people concerned.

Unfortunately, as we now know, the band were forced to leave the event as there were just too many people and it was obvious a lot of people were going to be unhappy.

Chaos broke out as people were in shock by the sudden turn of events. I think most of us really thought we were going to get in and meet the band and were probably quite naive to the reality of the situation.

At some point the line just unravelled, people were all over, and it became more of a damage control situation.

Everyone had brought personal items to get autographed and with the crush of people, it was a challenge to keep those items safe.

I'm 6 feet and 2 inches tall, so I held my painting above my head to keep it from getting damaged.

KROQ and The Wherehouse were called out for poor planning by Los Angeles City councilman Zev Yaroslavsky, and the news of the event was plastered all over the media.

It did seem a bit ridiculous that it was called "a riot".

It was really just a bunch of kids disappointed at not being able to meet their heroes after waiting all day in the warm California sunshine.

The event was obviously quite a successful launch for 'Violator' as the press was all over it.

Reflecting, 30 years on, I think it really was an ill-conceived plan. A band that had filled the Rose Bowl two years earlier were obviously going to draw a huge crowd.

This was the band's first studio release since that Rose Bowl concert and Southern California had become one of the largest Depeche Mode fan bases in the world.

I can't imagine that the band themselves foresaw this or I don't think they would have committed to it.

I wouldn't be surprised though if KROQ or the band's management, label reps, etc. considered the possibility.

The only ones to lose out were the fans as the majority of the crowd went home unhappy.

Still, my friends and I were undeterred in our quest to meet the band that night.

Earlier in the day, I had joked with some other fans in line that the band was going to be at the Cathouse after the event.

This was a heavy metal club put on by Riki Rachtman at the time. I had read in the LA Weekly some time before that the band were taken there once by Axl Rose.

So after the Wherehouse event got out of hand, I mentioned to my friends that perhaps there could be a possibility the band might show up there.

The club was held on Tuesday nights and the record signing just happened to fall on a Tuesday (20 March).

So we drove down to the club, by then located in a building called The Probe. And sure enough, parked across the street we saw their limos.

We waited until 2am for the bar to close since we were all underage. Sure enough, the first one to come stumbling out was Dave Gahan.

He was extremely intoxicated but quite friendly. He was wearing a white hoodie similar to one worn in the TV clip recorded for 'Enjoy The Silence' on the roof of the World Trade Center in New York City, and also seen in a 'Violator' promo poster.

I didn't ask him for his autograph but gave him a demo tape of my music. He was very thankful and stumbled his way to the limo. I also saw Andy Fletcher and gave him a demo tape as well.

One of my friends, her name is Viva, was talking to Alan Wilder and he invited her into the limo, but she didn't go. So although we didn't get any autographs, we were able to do what thousands were unable to do that infamous night and actually met the band.

Martin wasn't with them – it later emerged in an interview that he mentioned he was sick that night!

Chapter 7

Violating The World

"One look and you can see why Dodger Stadium was the coolest place to be that weekend on the whole fucking planet as that set-list is as close to a greatest hits or dream set as one could ever wish for at that point in Depeche Mode's career."

***

Today, of course, we look back on the 'Violator' era from a time when many bands regularly play arena tours on their first major tour.

Depeche Mode's live reputation was forged in a more traditional way: they had started playing local bars and discos and, through proper hard work, putting in backbreaking hours on tour in small vans and buses, the band built up a reputation as a standout live act that was arguably a stronger, more credible reputation than the one they had as a studio act.

The public face of Depeche Mode, the smiling, Saturday morning kids' show one, was very much at odds with the band's live persona.

The video 'The World We Live In And Live In Hamburg', recorded on the band's tour in support of 'Some Great Reward', is a prime example of just how powerful a live act Depeche Mode were in their early years.

In Europe, the band only regularly started playing arenas in 1986 on the 'Black Celebration' tour, five studio albums into their career. That tour saw them play their largest American tour to date with concerts at the likes of Radio City Music Hall and The Forum.

These were large venues for a band that, 'People Are People' aside, had made very little impact on the American charts.

Interestingly, the 'Music For The Masses' tour saw them play smaller venues again in their home country, with concerts at the likes of the Edinburgh Playhouse and Whitley Bay Ice Rink being played in the same month as shows at Wembley Arena and Birmingham NEC.

The North American leg of the tour, however, was entirely played in arenas until its famous culmination at the Rose Bowl on June 18 1988.

Essentially, by the end of the 'Music For The Masses' tour, Depeche Mode had, almost entirely by accident, become a stadium band. The concert at the Rose Bowl was the culmination of years of hard work, and the band's army of underground or alternative fans in America propelled the band to a level that even the most impartial of Depeche Mode observers could not have foreseen.

Alongside The Cure and New Order, Depeche Mode were part of a British invasion of a much different type than those that had gone before. This was not an invasion built on chart domination; this was a word-of-mouth invasion. An underground army of music fans was mobilised in support of these bands.

The Rose Bowl gig opened the door to the notion of an alternative band being able to stadia as the headline act.

The gig predated other huge tours by alternative acts such as R.E.M.'s 'Green World Tour' and The Cure's 'Prayer Tour'.

By the late 1980s, R.E.M. were the epitome of crossover success. The music media fell in love with them early, embracing their debut 'Murmur' fully, but the band's critical acclaim was not matched commercially until they crashed into the Billboard Top Ten in 1987 with 'The One I Love' from their breakthrough album 'Document'.

They let their relentless touring schedule spread the word and, by the time they joined Warners from independent label IRS in 1988, they were one of the biggest concert draws in the US despite their lack of commercial success, 'The One I Love' aside.

Their debut major label album 'Green' and the accompanying 'Green World Tour' took them into the arenas of the world, proving that the era's most renowned alternative act could stand toe to toe with their more commercial contemporaries such as U2.

Arguably, however, despite R.E.M.'s quite justified position as the decade's most lauded alternative band, Depeche Mode's Rose Bowl gig made R.E.M.'s transition to an arena band much easier. Depeche had made the idea that you didn't have to be a MOR or AOR band to play an arena or even a stadium acceptable.

The Cure's 'Prayer Tour' built on their Depeche Mode-like success in America. Perennial alternative favourites, The Cure had slowly built up a huge American following with 'Kiss Me, Kiss Me, Kiss Me' and 'Disintegration' joining 'Black Celebration' and 'Music For The Masses' as touchstones for legions of American teenagers.

The 'Prayer Tour' established The Cure as a *bona fide* arena band and, a year before Depeche Mode, they took the bold but ultimately entirely justified step of playing Dodger Stadium in Los Angeles.

Would that have been possible without Depeche Mode's Rose Bowl show? It seems unlikely, even improbable.

Depeche Mode had shown their contemporaries the way. They could play in large arenas and even stadiums. Why not? Why not have a (black) celebration on a mass scale?

Other less alternative bands such as U2 had managed it, too, doing it their own way and they were very much positioning themselves to sustain that. Could Depeche Mode do that though?

The 'World Violation Tour' proved that they could.

The 'Violator' album showed that Depeche Mode were more than comfortable with their new status.

Every song on the album brimmed with confidence, exuding a new sense of certainty. They were no longer singing from the perspective of being unlucky in love or needing a drink before they were anyone; from 'World In My Eyes' to 'Clean', Depeche were on the front foot, confident and ready to prove that they were fit to be considered one of the world's finest live acts.

The scale of World Violation matched this new, confident, ambitious Depeche Mode.

The tour production was on a scale hitherto unseen in Depeche Mode's case. 11 lorries transported the set around the world, backed up by a crew of close to 100 people and 88 dates were announced, taking in everywhere from Pensacola to Sydney to Birmingham (UK) and all points in between.

The band employed giant screens for the first time, projecting onto them what have become iconic Anton Corbijn films that perfectly complemented the live versions of the Violator tracks.

The use of bespoke films was unusual at the time for most bands, let alone acts perceived as alternative.

R.E.M. had incorporated film on their 1987 'Work' tour and the 'Green World Tour' made use of a screen more as a prop than as an accompaniment to the music, but they didn't use film as a part of the concert itself.

The 'World Violation Tour' took the notion of using the venue's sheer size as an opportunity to amplify the artistic statement to a new level. Corbijn's fellow clients U2 were certainly taking notes – their 'ZOO TV' tour took 'World Violation's blueprint and added several layers to it.

Depeche Mode's timing with 'World Violation' was perfect. The Cure were back in Europe having finished the American section of the 'Prayer Tour, R.E.M. were getting ready to dramatically change their sound with Out Of Time, New Order were very much doing other things post Technique and U2 had, to paraphrase Bono, gone away and were thinking it all up again.

The lack of activity on the part of these bands meant that Depeche Mode had a chance to capture the market for anyone who had an interest in alternative music.

'Violator' duly did that and the 'World Violation Tour' built on the impact the album had, making Depeche Mode one of, if not the biggest bands in the world in 1990.

Unusually for a Depeche Mode tour, 'World Violation' began in North America, breaking the band's habit of starting with a long stint in Europe. They had done this on each previous tour with the curious exception of the 'See You' tour in 1982, which saw the band open the tour at Crocs in Rayleigh before heading to New York for two shows at The Ritz.

The band rehearsed for the tour at Nomis Studios in London before they left for America and the opening concert at Pensacola in Florida at the city's Civic Center on May 28. The setlist that night proved to be the setlist for the whole tour – a collection of songs that only altered during Martin Gore's mid-set acoustic solo spot. On the opening night, the set comprised:

- Crucified / Kaleid
- World In My Eyes
- Halo
- Shake The Disease
- Everything Counts
- Master And Servant
- Never Let Me Down Again
- Waiting For The Night
- I Want You Now (Martin acoustic)
- World Full Of Nothing (Martin acoustic)

- Clean
- Stripped
- Policy Of Truth
- Enjoy The Silence
- Strangelove
- Personal Jesus
- Black Celebration (encore 1)
- A Question Of Time (encore 1)
- Behind The Wheel (encore 2)
- Route 66 (encore 2)

The set featured seven of Violator's nine tracks. Martin's acoustic set would feature the album's two remaining tracks, 'Sweetest Perfection' and 'Blue Dress' with the former appearing twenty times and the latter only twice, on July 31 at San Diego's Sports Arena and October 23 at Palais Omnisports de Paris-Bercy in the French capital.

In addition to those two tracks and the two tracks played on May 28, Martin's two-song acoustic set each night would also feature 'Here Is The House' and 'Little 15'.

At most of, if not every, show on the tour, concertgoers were greeted with two huge curtains featuring the DM logo seen on the front cover of the third 'Enjoy The Silence' 12-inch single smothering the stage as the taped intro of a mix of 'Crucified' and 'Kaleid' started.

While that track ended, the curtains would fall, revealing Martin, Andy and Alan on their tiered stage set as 'World In My Eyes' exploded into life with Dave wandering on a few seconds in, sending an already frenzied crowd into near hysteria.

Listening to recordings of concerts now or watching one of the sadly very few good videos there are, you really do get a sense of the sheer power of the crowds at the concerts. Depeche Mode fans are renowned for their sheer devotion to the band; 'World Violation's gigs illustrate that perfectly.

A 'Rolling Stone' article from June 1990 featured an interview with the band in Pensacola shortly before the tour began and the occasional comment about the May 28 show, mentioning the crowd that is "in a state of near pandemonium for the two hours Depeche are on stage" and a fan who spent $686 on the merchandise alone.

There was a sense of hysteria about the tour from the off, a hysteria that had been present from the signing session at The Wherehouse in Los Angeles.

As the tour progressed, the band's status grew. On the second date of the tour on May 30 at the Orlando Arena in Orlando, a local paper, 'The Orlando Sentinel', reported that the band had set a new record for per capita merchandise sales of $10.98, a record that stood until it was later broken by Garth Brooks.

Sell-out show followed sell-out show. The band played the first two-night stay of the tour on 9 and 10 June at Great Woods Amphitheater, Mansfield. It was followed by a second double header when they played two packed nights at The Spectrum in Philadelphia on June 13 and 14. It was received far less rapturously than earlier shows by Scott Brodeur of 'The Inquirer' than it was by the crowd.

Reviewing the first of the two shows, he bemoaned the band's ability to keep things "interesting musically," though he did note that the whole crowd, even on the third tier of the arena, was on its feet for the whole show.

The first major event of the tour was the show at Giants Stadium in New Jersey on June 16. It sold out within four hours of tickets going on sale. As on all concerts on the North American tour, the band were supported by Nitzer Ebb.

The Jesus and Mary Chain were added to the bill for this one show. There were nearly 50,000 people in attendance including the likes of Eddie Murphy and Sylvester Stallone. Flood was there too.

In 2011, he told 'Sonicstate' that he was introduced backstage to Adam Clayton and Bono who asked him to work with them on the strength of the work he'd done with Depeche Mode. 'Violator' and the 'World Violation' tour were already proving to be hugely influential.

The first of four concerts in Canada took place on June 21 at the Montreal Forum, a gig Alan recalled later in the tour as the concert with the loudest crowd. A planned Canadian show at the Civic Centre in Ottawa was cancelled when blue asbestos was discovered in the ceiling of the venue. It was felt that the risk to the band, crew and fans was too great to allow the concert to proceed.

Merchandise sales continued to go through the roof with the 'Detroit Free Press' reporting on July 10 1990 that the June 26 gig at Blossom Music Center in Cuyahoga Falls "broke the 18-year record… for the greatest number of t-shirts and sweatshirts sold during any rock concert."

Footage from the two concerts at World Music Theatre in Chicago was used for the 'World In My Eyes' video, giving a tantalising glimpse of the sheer scale of the concerts.

The first problem with the tour occurred on July 24. A sold-out outdoor show at Park West Amphitheater in Park City, Utah, was scheduled but it had to be cancelled due to torrential rain.

Happily, the band was able to quickly reschedule, and they played the Salt Palace Arena in Salt Lake City the next night, July 25. As Alan recalled on the 'Violator' reissue documentary, the hastily arranged "makeshift gig" on July 25 "was one of the best shows we ever played." The band used their surprise free time in Park City to shoot additional footage used on 'Strange Too' at a drive-in movie theatre.

The band played three sold-out nights at San Diego Sports Arena on July 28, 29 and 31, becoming, according to the 'Times-Advocate Newspaper' in its end-of-year review, only the second act to ever sell out three consecutive nights at that venue after Neil Diamond.

The North American leg of the gig ended on a huge high with two sold-out shows at Los Angeles' Dodger Stadium on August 4 and 5. The first concert was announced on June 2 and all 48,175 tickets sold out within half an hour of going on sale.

This led to the second concert being announced on June 5 and, again, every single ticket was snapped up. Given that Depeche Mode regularly plays stadia in the 21st Century, it is perhaps hard to contemplate just how impressive a feat this was in 1990.

Bear in mind that only nine years earlier they had played Rafters in Manchester on August 5, 1981.

Suddenly finding themselves playing to nearly 100,000 people at a baseball stadium over two sold-out nights was quite remarkable.

As well as Nitzer Ebb, the band were supported by Electronic, the group then recently formed by New Order's Bernard Sumner and Johnny Marr of The Smiths. The Dodger's concerts were the duo's live debut and in a quite marvellous move, they were joined by Pet Shop Boys, whose Neil Tennant had provided vocals on a couple of tracks on Electronic's self-titled debut album.

The UK press attended the concerts with 'Sounds' noting that "50,000 maniacs" had " a hell of a good time."

UK television show 'The Word' also featured a report about the gig. The press in the band's home country was finally, albeit reluctantly, acknowledging that Depeche Mode were very much a big deal.

The band left North America having sold nearly two million copies of 'Violator' and having redefined the notion of a stadium act.

Following a three-week break, 'World Violation' moved to Australia for the band's first-ever concerts in that country. Dave's voice had developed a problem, however, and so the first show at Horden Pavilion in Sydney was a shorter version of the show that had toured North America, with the encore's 'Black Celebration' and 'A Question Of Time' dropped from the setlist.

Australian band Boxcar were the support act at the concert. Dave's voice only worsened after the concert, leading to Depeche Mode taking the highly unusual step of cancelling a gig.

The planned September 1 show at Melbourne's Festival Hall became unique in the band's history by being the first concert they had ever cancelled due to ill health.

Dave recovered in time for the band to play six shows in Japan, with the first taking place on September 4 at Shimin Kaikan in Fukuoka. The setlist returned to the 20-song set seen on the North American tours and, for all six shows in Japan, there was no support act.

A unique four-track CD featuring the four 'Violator' singles was released to celebrate the tour. Packaged in a 'snap pack' sleeve, the CD was given away to concert-goers at the Japanese concerts and it remains a highly collectable and extremely rare piece of Depeche Mode merchandise.

The band then played concerts in Kobe, Kanazawa and Nagoya, with the setlists at the latter two the briefer 18-song set as played in Sydney. The Japanese tour concluded on September 11 and 12, with two concerts at Nippon Budokan in Tokyo with a full 20-song set played on the first night and the encore featuring 'Black Celebration' and 'A Question Of Time' omitted on night two.

After a two-week break, the band returned to Europe to begin the final leg of the tour, starting at Forest National in Brussels.

The support act for the entire European leg of the tour was the German synthpop group Electribe 101.

After Brussels, the band played their first two German shows of the tour at the Westfalenhalle in Dortmund on September 29 and 30. By this point in their career, Depeche Mode had a huge German fanbase and that remains the case to this day.

In 1990, the band's popularity was of course at a peak worldwide; in Germany the reaction to Depeche Mode was frenzied.

'Select', a UK music magazine, ran a four-page special based on the Dortmund concerts. Andrew Harrison wrote, "Believe it or not, World Violation is, first and foremost, a rock 'n' roll show on a panoramic scale. Perhaps it's just the volume or the shock of finding such solitary music in a context of size and excess, but in 1990, Depeche Mode win by simple power. It's not simply stunning – at times it's frightening."

The tour crisscrossed the continent, moving from Germany to Denmark and Sweden and then back into Germany and France. At the Frankfurt Festhalle show on October 8, the former number one ranked tennis player Steffi Graf danced by the side of the stage.

Graf, who was famously pictured at a tournament earlier in the year wearing a long-sleeved 'Violator' t-shirt, was Fletch's idol at the time, according to an interview he gave to 'NME' on November 3. He seemed delighted that she had turned up at the concert.

The show in Lyon on October 11 attracted a crowd of around 23,000, according to Daryl Bamonte's 'World Violation' tour diary in 'Bong', the Depeche Mode fan club magazine.

Billie Rae Martin recalls that the crowd at that gig were very receptive to Electribe 101, noting that "the Lyon audience was kind and jumped up and down throughout our set, which was a most welcome surprise."

This reaction was a surprise for the band as they had not been treated very well by the hardcore Depeche Mode fanbase – a fanbase noted in those days for their impatient reaction to support bands generally.

Martin recalls objects frequently being thrown at the band. By the time the tour reached Paris for three sold-out nights at Palais Omnisports de Paris-Bercy, the reaction to the support band had become so terrible that she refused to appear on the second night.

After Paris, the tour moved between Germany, The Netherlands and France before moving to Spain and Italy with gigs in Barcelona, Madrid, Milan and Rome, with a show in Marseilles thrown in for good measure between Madrid and Milan.

Bamonte's 'World Violation' tour diary in 'Bong 12' noted that the band's assistant tour accountant Mark Aurelio was arrested after a fight broke out between him and some local ticket touts. The promoter had made 200 extra tickets available for the concert and Mark duly set about selling them legitimately, much to the displeasure of the local touts. Mark ended up being blamed by local police.

The concert in Rome on November 12 saw the first European appearance of the abbreviated setlist first seen in Sydney, with the first encore featuring 'Black Celebration' and 'A Question

Of Time' dropped. The band then returned to France for two nights in Bordeaux before they finished the continental leg of 'World Violation' at Parc De Penfeld in Brest.

The last six dates of the tour took place in England. The band had previously toured the UK extensively on each tour, but this time restricted their appearances to three sold-out shows each at Wembley Arena in London and the NEC in Birmingham, with a combined audience of around 70,000 people. The UK music press turned out *en masse* to review the concerts.

In the 'NME', Paul Lester wrote of the first Wembley Arena gig, "'Personal Jesus' inspires an astonishing display of audience participation, wherein every single last person in the Arena holds their arms aloft and chants 'Reach out and touch faith!'… [The crowd's] glassy-eyed submission takes on a beauty that only those who are present can appreciate."

Adam Sweeting in 'The Guardian' noted that "the final section of the show was akin to a celebration." In his London Evening Standard review of the Wembley Arena gig, Spencer Bright said, "Their concert at Wembley Arena was akin to an evangelical meeting such was the devotion of the saluting crowd," adding that, "Depeche Mode astonishingly seem as if they are yet to peak."

The conclusion of the tour brought an end to the band's most successful, high-profile tour to date. They had reached a height that few other bands reach and it seemed like there was nothing that could stop them from capitalising on this and becoming even bigger.

For the first time in their career, Depeche Mode took some real time off and went their separate ways to recuperate and plan the next move.

Andy Franks (UK), production director for the 'World Violation' Tour

'Music For The Masses' - that was a pretty long tour, like eight or nine months, maybe a year. It's all a much longer period than most people are aware as they just see them once the album has come out. They don't appreciate how much work has gone into that.

What was slightly different after '101' was the film, which had been shot and then had to be edited and that took quite a bit of time.

There were quite a lot of trips to and from New York to go to editing suites and bits for them to look at and approve. I actually think they gave a pretty free-reign to D. A. Pennebaker and just let him get on with it because that's obviously his sort of skill: to put the weeks of footage that he'd managed to shoot into some cohesive sort of project really.

So there was that, plus the writing and the preparations for 'Violator', so it kind of all meshed from one thing into the other, and before we knew it had all really a few years had passed and then we were off again.

J.D. Fanger and I were full-time employees for the band, so even when they weren't on tour we were sort of in the office and you were aware of things. I mean obviously, they were doing their studio work and, to some extent, we never really went along to the studio. We occasionally organised a curry to be sent from London to somewhere or other!

It was more bits and pieces like that – but there was definitely the feeling that something special was coming. I think with any band, when they are releasing an album, they never quite know how it's going to be perceived and that's always a worry but there was certainly, I would say, a feeling around the inner sanctum of people – their publicist, Daniel and others – that there was something special happening.

Alan was always known to be the one with the greatest musical and production abilities, with his background. I think he'd learned a lot in the last few years with the band and all the ducks were lining up in a row. It was the culmination of all sorts of stuff, with him and Flood feeding off each other

I remember hearing 'Personal Jesus' and thinking, "Fucking hell! They go from being three synthesisers and a vocalist to that?"

When they first started, people used to not see them as a band because they didn't have a drummer. In fact, when we first toured in America, local stagehands didn't want to load the equipment into the van because they said, "Well, you're not a real band without a drummer so we are not loading your gear in!"

It was that kind of thing for a long time and suddenly having a guitar playing at the front of one of the new songs seemed to be like such a movement from where they first started to be almost rock band.

It was very surprising but, also, what a tune!

Alan was okay to play the drums, which was something that was unheard of and, in fact, a lot of Depeche purists weren't keen on it, thinking they should sort of just be synthesisers and everything should be programmed.

But they were getting much more into playing live instruments on stage and wanted to have a much more diverse sound.

I still think Martin is one of the great guitar players. He never ever would mention it but his solos - a bloke who plays two or three notes but it's like the best two or three notes you've ever heard. I think he is the master of understatement when it comes to guitar playing.

With some bands, when they are on the road, they are writing all the time or there's a lot of creativity going on, but Depeche were never one of those bands.

For them, going out on the road was the culmination of, "We've done all that fucking hard work and recording the album and everything like that, now let's get out and play the songs and party," which was why they were there in the first place.

Probably at least a year or more in advance, we would know that they are going on tour, a rough idea of when the tour is, and when the album is going to be finished.

Then, when dates start to go on sale and are promoted and discussed with them. Then you have the framework of the touring schedule and the places you are going to play, then you start thinking about the production you are going to put into it

Maybe up to 15 months ahead of the tour, we were starting to put people in place and having meetings with stage set designers. Anton was becoming much more involved in this kind of thing as well, so it was quite a long time in advance.

Very few bands will set off and say, "Okay, we are going to go on tour for 140 shows." Instead, you think, "We are going to go on tour and if we can get three or four months out of it then that would be good."

But they sell out straight away, so suddenly there's more mileage and, of course, promoters want you to do more, so it's a case of looking at it and working out how far. But I don't think anybody envisaged that the tour was going to be that long really. It got that to that length because of the success of the shows really.

You can't just throw in an extra day, because you've got to make sure the dates are available and you've also got to ensure that you can logistically get from one place to another. We say we are going to tour Europe for two months or something like that, then you plan the European tour and then you go to the United States for, maybe, two or three months, but then not necessarily back to Europe.

***

They've always been at the cutting edge. technology-wise, with the instruments that they've had.

I can remember when the Emulator – the first computerised keyboard – came out. When we would fly to shows it had its own spot on the plane. We got it a ticket, called it Emulator and it used to travel the world with us in a very comfy seat.

They were always looking for the latest equipment that they could use. When it was the very early days, they'd go out with just a four-track tape recorder, then a 48-track digital machine that would play the backing track – so everything was getting sort of very big.

From the songs that they wanted to perform, they would then work out how they were going to perform them, which would all be done at a band rehearsal maybe five or six weeks prior to a tour, where they would go through it all, working out which songs they were going to do.

They would get the samples and various bits and pieces on all those songs and sometimes, on older songs, they would use a newer remix of it, so they would have quite a few weeks in rehearsals working out how all it went before they got into production rehearsal.

Alan was the musical one, the creative side of it, working out how it would best be done, and which bits would work. They had everything on tape but it was very important to play live as well, so it was incorporating that and the triggers and various samples and live instruments – and who is doing what bit.

Martin was getting to the stage where he quite enjoyed playing the guitar. He'd always been kind of a shy personality, so coming out from behind the keyboard was a big step for him.

***

We did production rehearsals in Pensacola, Florida.

So there was the banter that we'd been there for quite a while and Anton was involved and Richard [Bell]... So, the band turned up after a particularly long flight, after connecting from somewhere. Alan just walked up and said, "Is that the best you could do? Let's go to the pub!" I was like, "Great, thank you very much!"

I think it was a Hilton hotel that had been built at the back of a train station – it was very bizarre. It was like walking into an old railway station and then there was a hotel there.

It was quite a large stage set and I remember, when we were going to go to Japan, where we were only doing three or four shows, it didn't make sense to ship it out.

So we took loads of photos – I mean hundreds and hundreds and hundreds of photos of the stage set. The Japanese promoter sent a guy over to measure everything up, so when we went to Japan and walked into the first gig, there was an identical stage set. Except they hadn't quite got it.

There's always something that's a little bit awry, so it wasn't quite as high as our usual one, so to get all the cables and monitors, this poor guy had to crawl underneath it. I don't know how he got through it – he had to be just eight inches high to crawl through all the stuff there, but they gave us the stage that they made out of steel and they transported it around for us.

It was absolutely incredible! And the band thought it was the same stage – painted and everything. It was done exactly the same, except that it was made out of steel and ours was made out of aluminium.

In Japan, they don't allow smoke machines – they were something that was banned and we weren't sure what was going to happen. But suddenly, we saw 200 guys outside with black bin liners they were filling up to use as a smoke machine. So they were shaking the bags to let the smoke out into the stage – it was absolutely brilliant!

It would have been around 80 people on the tour, with ten trucks, four or five buses, all the crew such as eight or nine in the lighting department, seven or eight on the sound, there were video people – it was, you know, just massive.

I was the production director so it was my responsibility to ensure that we got into all the buildings. We had production managers and a team that were working out all the logistics to ensure that we were in and out of everywhere.

It's actually a little bit easier because once you get to that level, especially when you are playing in America, where you know the sports arenas that they have are used to productions being put in and it's all multi-purpose.

When you are in the UK, it was certainly harder because there was only Wembley Arena around in those days. There was the Birmingham NEC but that was a sort of a novelty. It was built in such a way that the ceiling was designed for an exhibition centre, but not really with the thought of putting concerts on.

We had a clearance of about 30-40 feet to the ceiling but once you've taken all the rigging that you need to hang all your lights then everything is just above your head!

Touring Europe was more of an issue than touring America because there you would turn up, set up and away you go. There was a lot of organisation but the running of it basically was like taking a small town of people and equipment away. When you think of a few trucks worth of gear, loading it and out of the venue every day – it's quite a feat.

We also did Giants stadium, which was pretty cool because we did that and then we did Radio City Music Hall afterwards.

I think it was a charity show but Radio City Music Hall had the nickname at the time of "Union", when the unions were really strong – those that were running the shows were brutally hard on crews, particularly if you were an English band. They could make or break you!

But it means that you create a relationship with them, so we turned up after doing Giants Stadium with 35 trucks' worth of stuff. I think they were just so bemused by the madness and the wacky Brits that we all got on and we had a fantastic time there!

I remember at Los Angeles Dodger Stadium the band had sold out the two nights and were offered a third night but because the 'diamond at the stadium (where the pitcher with the baseball stands) could only be covered up for a certain amount of time, so the third show would then have to be on sale for August 3, which was before the original dates.

This meant that the people who bought the tickets for the third show would actually be the first ones to see the band play and so the band refused to do it because they said it wouldn't be fair on their fans.

I think that personifies the kind of band that they were and also the fact that at the time they didn't really have management as such, so they were calling their own shots a lot more. Most of the heavyweight managers of this world would have told the bands, "Fuck it, you are going to fucking do it guys!"

***

Depeche Mode are the masters of the understatement. Martin always seemed to have said that he didn't want to write songs that were popular because that's not why he wrote his songs – there was always this anti feeling because that's not why they were doing it.

They were doing it because they wanted to do what they wanted to do and, therefore, did everything in their own way.

They all measure success in different sorts of ways but I do think that they must have been happy about the tour and going out and seeing those fans. The experience of a gig and seeing the people that are there – the mad fans that know all the words and then you see everybody.

Dave was your typical frontman but he never used to speak to the audience apart from a "C'mon!" or "Hey you!" – there was never any rapport that he used to have with the audience.

You were either in or you were out. If you were in, there was this incredible feeling that you were part of something that was just amazing. I'm sure the band used to feel that as well and absolutely love it – I mean they must have!

They've always been lucky because they have not been the sort of people that get recognised. They didn't do all the chatshows so they could still go about their lives with a certain amount of normality.

The fans were always amazing. I remember somebody walking past Robbie Williams when I was with him once, trying to get to me because they remembered me from '101' – it's that kind of stuff and yet the outside world just isn't aware of it. You are part of an elite private gang that's got its own little world and we always felt like that when we were touring around.

I remember in 1987 and 1988, the first time we got a private plane, we had this propeller thing and Pink Floyd were also on tour at that time. We used to park our plane underneath the wing of theirs because it seemed like a funny thing to do. Depeche were just this little entity that was going about their own business, in their own little world.

***

When they used to go on the road it was a party atmosphere and they kind of were used to it. We got into a routine of we'd do the show and then we'd all go out and party.

The drug scene was changing. Ecstasy was coming in and there were big parties, plus their music led them into that kind of thing as well.

We'd go to a party somewhere, and crawl back to the hotel at about seven or eight in the morning. You'd have a few hours to get on the plane and fly to the next place and that was the cycle really. It was very much a hedonistic lifestyle I think, perhaps surprisingly… but then it was a different sort of world back then. There weren't all these restrictions that there are around now.

You can't move now without having police looking at you and all the security measures at airports. In those days, you just turned up and got on a plane and flew somewhere – happy days, really.

Now there are all sorts of security at nightclubs. They are so security conscious these days but in those days it wasn't – it was a very hedonistic sort of thing. It was still pre-AIDS, well

AIDS was just around – again, it was that sort of lifestyle where people were very free. It was almost like after the summer of love of the 1960s but with ecstasy.

The band were not yet going their separate ways but certainly had their own ways.

They were individuals and there used to be a certain element of partying and whatever but they also actually partied with their friends. They were always very sociable people. We used to come back to a hotel and they would buy the drinks for people and we'd go out to a club and they were very generous and very sociable people

It was during 'Violator' when we had our first ghetto blaster for the dressing rooms – a mobile sound system, really, and after the show, they used to party. It wasn't that they got off the stage and into the limos and were gone. The crew would be banging on the door saying that the trucks needed to go and could we please get the ghetto blaster into the truck so we could head to the next place. The band would actually be the last ones at the gig, rather than the crew.

But with any band, when you've been together for a long time, things are going to come up. You are family and living on the road is a very special situation and you have to have a very special relationship because you are living very closely.

You've got to remember what living on the road is like for these guys. They've been on the road for six to nine months a year, living together, doing an album, so they were probably in each other's faces for a very long time.

You know with a family, when everybody goes on holiday for a week or two, by the end of it you are like, "Fucking hell – I want to go off and do my own thing!" because you've all been together in an intensity that you are not used to. Multiply that for a year and add in drinks and drugs and it can be quite a tough environment

I mean everyone is pretty exhausted and you want to get home to friends and family and you know it's the finishing line, but it is uphill, with obstacles and a couple of water jumps and it's raining and it's getting colder because it's getting back to England in the fall.

It usually is a bit of a trudge, but again tours often end up with everybody always wanting to do a big show at the end just to remember it and to take them up to the next stage. It's always the sort of thing which is good from the band's point of view, but which is a pain in the ass for the production people.

Once you've run a marathon, it's very hard if someone comes up to you and says, "When are you doing your next marathon?"

All the talk of drugs and the rest of it – the drug of appearing on stage in front of 50-60 000 people is a pretty strong sort of thing and anybody would struggle to go back to normal life.

But I think because they've always been a pretty down-to-earth group of people, even though they were getting into the private plane thing. They were still basic people and I think they were always surprised by their success.

They had been growing for ten years to build themselves, they toured relentlessly, so they built themselves up to that level. 'Violator' was finally the icing on the cake because all the other ingredients were there and the cake had risen beautifully in the oven.

François Kevorkian (USA), studio mixer on 'Violator'

Until I actually saw Depeche Mode live on the tour, I don't think that I actually understood the potency of Dave's charm as a vocalist.

I would say this not just as a fan, but as a fan of many bands with strong frontmen – he is, I think, an unheralded frontman.

In the modern music era, he's very underrated as a performer.

The fact that it's an electronic band in a live setting - you've got three guys behind keyboards that are relatively static – yet he has the ability to command an entire audience, just by what he does.

It's always been something that really struck me.

Blessed with an incredible voice but being able to perform night after night with huge crowds of 10, 20, 30 or 60,000 all going along for the ride with him.

But when I saw the live show, I was gobsmacked by Martin. I say this truthfully, as I have experienced this very few times in my entire life.

I went to see the Michael Jackson tour at the height of his popularity when 'Thriller' was out, and it was total hysteria.

But more than the most incredible time I had when watching Jackson was when the Depeche set got stripped down to nothing but Martin's voice, in a ballad, with few instruments.

When Martin did a song by himself, with just an acoustic guitar, I thought, "Well, I never got to see John Lennon but I got to see you. And that's good enough for me."

I even told him – he was so emotional!

Seeing things like that, made me feel that those are the things do change your life. He was definitely the kind of person that was capable of doing that.

Not so much on the record, for me, for some reason. But when I saw Martin play live – wow!

I don't think that even by mixing the record and being in the studio with them, I had realised how it would translate in front of a big audience.

I mean, of course, you could say, "Well, part of the factor there is that the audience is adoring them. They love those songs and they know them like the back of their hand."

It goes beyond that. I'm talking about magnetism. That special thing between the performer and the audience that makes it so unique.

Richard Bell (New Zealand), video producer for the 'Violator' singles and tour backdrops

The tour visuals were what got us to go to America in the first place.

They wanted footage to play on screens while they were playing live. It had to be done in America because the band were in America, rehearsing, and the tour was going to start there.

We also needed to film the final videos, too.

It would have been a nightmare to try to do it in Europe. You would have been forever shipping stuff around.

The band by then were completely trusting Anton, visually.

So, they said, "Hey Anton, c'mon give us some ideas, give us some thoughts?"

It was very random, the way it was pulled together. We were shooting a bit of this for one song, then a bit of that for another, as well as the single videos – but it was all part of the same package.

The cowgirls for *Personal Jesus* live were filmed in the same studio as when we did the *Policy of Truth* video.

It was a constantly moving thing – we'd say, "Well, okay, we're in this city, we've got the band for two days, so we can do this bit of video, we can do this bit of projection and we can do that. And then we'll go here and we'll meet up and we'll do this and edit that and shoot this."

It probably made life a little bit easier for them, because we could join shoots together. We could be shooting a bit of this and doing this video at the same time or this projection footage can go into this video because it already exists.

By handling the whole thing, it made sense in a purely practical process, let alone the aesthetic process.

But we were also switching equipment a lot as we couldn't shoot Super 8 for the projection. They were all 35mm films. It took months and months to do.

At the time, Pink Floyd aside, Depeche were way up there in terms of technology for the tour.

We were synchronising video and film – that hadn't really been done before, with 35mm projectors running.

I came up with the way of switching everything on, simultaneously. This was all new, so much so that I went to Australia on the tour, because nobody would know how to get it to work.

It was relatively straightforward. But I remember we had to have specific cogs manufactured to go into the projectors and run them at exactly the right speed. And then there was a sync system that we could hit with projectors on and at very set moments.

Now it would be dead easy – some computer would send a trigger to all the various devices and they would all come on together, but this was way before that.

It was a question of actually physically turning knobs at the right moment, triggered by a visual cue that we had embedded inside the video. So it was quite complex!

We went to Pensacola in Florida with them, for the rehearsal.

My wife actually packed in her job in England and came out – because I was relatively recently married and she got bored of me being away for so long.

So she lived with us in LA, came to Pensacola and came to New York. There wasn't a month where we weren't with the band for a few days, leading up to or during the tour.

I always remember that going on tour with Depeche was one of the big highlights.

It was always good fun, they had a good road crew, and they were super well organised. Andy Franks was as one of the best tour managers I've come across. J. D. Fanger was also around and it was a good vibe.

They do the hard yards, they have to perform every night and you just go watch it and have a good time and drink the beer, provided the bit that you set up works correctly.

I remember I always got on really well got on with the whole band.

And they all got on fine then. I'm sure that if you went back through, you could find a day or a moment, where Anton would say, "Rich, you screwed up on this production," and then I'd run around like a madman trying to solve the problem that I created.

I think Dave is a phenomenal performer but he carried the show. With all due respect to the others, a large part of their time on stage, they were stuck behind keyboards.

There were always efforts to work out ways to get them out but for a large part of time, they physically had to be behind keyboards.

For example, Jimmy Page and Robert Plant of Led Zeppelin, the fans can't go, "Oh what's Jimmy Page doing, let's go back to Robert Plant" – that just doesn't exist with Depeche.

You've got Dave to look at. That's why the films and the projections happened. They realised we needed to add something to this.

But Dave is an absolute stellar performer. Night-in, night-out, he knew exactly how to put a show on, give everybody a good time and do his best.

Billie Ray Martin (Germany), singer with Electribe 101, support act in Europe on the 'World Violation Tour'

The band asked us to support. Our record company was contacted and told us. It was not some record company-generated idea but came from the group, who liked our music enough to invite us.

They also offered us some support money for the tour, which is not usually done. A very kind gesture from them. Hence we had some support from our record company and there was some money from Depeche Mode for us, too.

I seem to remember that it was quite short notice. We had enough time to prepare, rehearse, program etc. in our studio in Birmingham. So perhaps it was about a month or two's notice.

The 'Violator' album is really what turned DM into a religion (which in Germany to this day they still are).

Great songwriting and seminal production from Flood. It's sort of the ultimate DM album I guess, although for me personally, I love some of the earlier albums just as much.

Because the tour was not an easy one for us to be on, we kind of made fun of having to hear the same opening notes and basslines to the tour each day. We just had to laugh sometimes about stuff so we could sing the beginning notes of certain songs. But they were so iconic and we witnessed the crowds going nuts each day just hearing a synth opening.

We would even wake up in a hotel somewhere, switch on the radio, and there was the same opening to the song we would hear later during soundchecks and the show. I would turn the radio up massively loud for the rest of the band, in their hotel rooms, to get a taste of what was to come. It always got a laugh from the other group members, unless I woke them up.

We would be canned off stage at most shows. But in Lille, the audience was kind and jumped up and down throughout our set, which was a most welcome surprise.

Berlin and Paris stood out as the most horrible shows, in terms of sheer hate thrown at us by these people. In Paris, I refused to go on for the second date, and the other band members had to deal with tomatoes thrown at them without me. I just could not face it.

In Hamburg, people acted much more kind and civilised. But the rest of Europe was tough for us. Being back in the UK and performing the big shows there was a breath of fresh air because people behaved normally and enjoyed our show. No incidents there!

There are many stories that can be told of how we were treated by an audience that did not want to listen to a support group. It was not about our music.

In Paris, on the second day, Alan Wilder actually went on stage before the Electribe 101 group members went on, without me that day, to tell the audience that the group had personally invited us and to be kind.

Our band suffered throughout this tour to the point where we really did not get on anymore, as the strain and the pressure were too much to take. We didn't last long as a group after the tour, not just because of the tour, but it was part of it.

We had hate thrown at us and everything from tomatoes to coins. It was horrible and I couldn't work out why people would behave this way. I was a young singer who wanted to do just that: sing. To be faced with thousands of distorted faces, screaming at you and making rude gestures is not something any band expects.

When you're on stage you only see the first, say, 20 rows, and that's where the die-hard fans are who are there to get the support group off stage. Horrible. I started drinking after a while. Luckily this did not continue after the tour.

It was the toughest time for me and the rest of the band, as we did not expect what we found ourselves faced with.

Dave was most kind and we shared the odd laugh in the corridors before they would go on, and we could come off stage.

However, the tour, as far as technicalities were concerned, went smoothly. We didn't get much of a soundcheck, although we played fully live and DM used playback for most of what they were doing.

It was a bit tough at times to see Dave walk up and down the stage going, "One-two, one-two," when we could have used a bit more time for checking our sound. We played fully live, even the electronically programmed stuff was mixed from a live desk each night.

I don't remember fans being at the afterparties. There was usually a selection of a small number of people. I didn't attend many parties as I keep myself to myself as a rule. I do remember a couple of parties where I enjoyed dancing with everyone. It was a time when Dave was not very well. I remember seeing him not feeling too great among the other group members and I really felt for him.

He was always kind and fun though and definitely made the best of the situation he found himself in. I remember Dave sitting alone during dinners or with the crew, as the rest of the group would not sit with him. It was sad to see.

I think we could all see, and certainly, DM were aware, of how big the whole thing was. Dave during this time did not cope too well with the situation he found himself in.

To his great credit, he put on the most incredible show each and every night. Just amazing what kind of energy he could put into his performance.

The crew on the tour was all-male in those days (except catering and merch), which was odd. No one ever spoke to me or engaged with me, as I guess I was not fitting the 'norm' of a female in terms of the way I presented myself. So I was ignored. It was an incredibly lonely time for me.

There was a lot of 'male' behaviour from the crew that even the Electribe 101 guys found a bit alienating, but I believe nowadays there is more of a mix of people on these tours.

I do believe the group knew how to shield themselves from fans when they needed to, and I did witness them doing so at times, telling people politely that at this time they would not sign autographs.

Because my last name is Martin, fans would ring my hotel room at all hours of the night, hoping to speak to Martin Gore. I swore at a lot of people down the phone and ended up checking in under different names!

Mistie Fowlkes (USA), daughter of the owner of the drive-in movie theatre featured in the video for 'World In My Eyes'

I was 14 at the time when Depeche Mode came to film their video at our Drive-In Theatre.

I remember my father coming home from work and he said, "Mistie, I think one of your bands wants to make a video at the Drive-In. I was so excited and couldn't imagine what band he was talking about.

He didn't pay attention to my music – just said I listened to "funeral music" and to turn it down. I asked him which band and he tried to say Depeche Mode but totally butchered the name.

When I asked him if he was talking about Depeche Mode and he said, "Yes," I couldn't believe it. He said a man got a hold of him in regards to using the Drive-In because of the background of the mountain and screen.

He said he was probably going to do it because we could use the money. I told him there was *no* probably about it, he was doing it and I was going to be there along with my brother.

My father really didn't have to prepare anything other than put up the words 'Strange Too' on the sign, the way they wanted.

I believe it took two days but the band was only there one night – the first night. The band arrived in limos and the convertible used was rented from a local tortilla company. There were also RVs (recreational vehicles) for the band to go into and relax in between filming.

We were not aware of the storyline but really wondered since they made a makeshift bed behind the snack bar. We watched them film as he tossed and turned on the silk sheets with the toy car. So freaking awesome! We figured it would be something like a dream sequence but didn't know for sure.

After a few takes of Dave driving into the theatre with the model, the sun began to set and it was time to eat. They had it catered with tables, food, etc.

I can't remember what kind of food for the life of me, I was too excited to eat. My brother just sat and stared at the band eating! There were several round tables with tablecloths set up in the middle of the drive-in, off to the left side of the snack bar. The RVs were in front of the tables.

The filming process must have taken from around 7pm to midnight, give or take.

The band wandered around in the snack bar. My brother and I made hot dogs for the non-vegetarians and gave them anything they wanted. They drank Corona with limes. I can't remember doing anything more nerve-racking than making hot dogs for Depeche Mode and speaking to them like normal people.

The band were kind and would speak to us, we just didn't know what to say, we were so starstruck, we probably just drooled. They asked us questions about the drive-in and we answered the best we could!

My brother and I snuck into one of the RVs and took some empty Corona bottles and a piece of chewed gum. We kept the bottles but my brother sold the gum to a girl at school that next school year and she put the gum in her mouth, chewed and said it was just like kissing Dave Gahan!

We told our friends about the filming and their friends told their friends and so on. There was a place across the street where people gathered with binoculars to try and see the band.

I remember waving at them and they screamed and yelled. Then we got in trouble for causing a ruckus during filming. We quickly stopped because we weren't about to risk our place in the middle of the most amazing evening of our lives.

We received free tickets to a show but had prior engagements and couldn't make it. We were heartbroken!

The finished product was even better than what we imagined it would be. Having all the videos strung together with our theatre was the most amazing thing to watch. We watched it over and over again with our friends until the videotape went bad.

Niggels Uhlenbruch (Germany), fan and DJ

1990 was a crucial year for Germany: It was the year of the reunion of East and West Germany, and Depeche Mode's 'Violator' was released.

I'm not trying to say that both events were on the same historic level in general terms, of course. And it is very obviously an over-simplification.

But if you ask an East German DM fan – the term 'devotee didn't exist back then – there is a good chance that he or she will say that the fall of the wall and the release of 'Violator' and all things around it, in particular the tour, were *both life-changing* events. And they were more intertwined than you might guess.

The years 1989 and 1990 were certainly very interesting and exciting times for Germany! On November 9 1989, the Berlin Wall came down and marked the beginning of the end of the Cold War.

Almost the entire year of 1990 was dominated by a somewhat rushed but peaceful reunification process of the two German states, the Federal Republic of Germany in the west and the German Democratic Republic in the east. This process culminated in German unity on October 3 1990.

It was the turn of an era not only for Germany but for the entire world, as the fall of the Berlin Wall marked the end of the Cold War.

Just as much as 'Violator' was the turn of an era for Depeche Mode and their fans in their little Depeche-y world – a world which was not so little anymore! Depeche Mode turned into global superstars in the years 1987 to 1990, they broke the US market with 'Music For The Masses', became an unlikely stadium act with '101', and the immense success of 'Violator' catapulted them even higher to global superstardom.

In the decade prior to the collapse of the Eastern Bloc, Depeche Mode grew from Cold War kids to glitzy superstars worldwide.

All of a sudden, seemingly, Depeche Mode were the biggest act around!

In some places, however, DM had been superstars for a number of years already, and Germany was certainly one of these.

Depeche had solid success here in their early years and with 'People Are People' they hit the number one spot in the German singles chart, making them a teenage sensation and a high-grossing live act. 'People Are People' remained their only number one in Germany for a long time – until 'Dream On' in 2001, in fact – but the overall popularity of DM increased from year to year and from album to album.

The success of 'Violator' in 1990 might have seemed like a sudden explosion in some other parts of the world but in Germany, it was the result of a long and unstoppable process.

That the band chose to premier 'Enjoy The Silence' months ahead of its release at a rather odd German TV show is quite telling! It was 'Peter's Pop-Show', an annual media event with lots of acts lip-syncing to playback, which was recorded at the huge Westfalenhalle in Dortmund on November 17 1989, and aired on December 2. If you want to get an idea of how big DM already were in Germany at that time then just rewatch the performance.

Mind you, this was not a pure DM crowd but a 15,000-capacity venue with people coming to see a variety of artists, from Janet Jackson to Tina Turner and from Bonfire to, oh dear, the inevitable David Hasselhoff.

Interestingly Erasure and Camouflage were also on the bill, so some synthpop fans certainly ventured to witness the playback charade on location. Smile, you're on TV now!

Attending 'Peter's Pop-Show' never came to my mind back then, even though I didn't live too far away from Dortmund, but I just had started my own little adventure by reaching out to the east of our country, at first by finding penpals in the still existing GDR.

Just weeks ago this would have been near impossible but now it was easy. Just grab a teen magazine like 'Bravo' or 'Pop Rocky' and check the penpal section. Or, as in my case, the 'New Life Sound', a magazine that did have its name for a reason as it started as a Swiss DM fanzine and evolved into an underground music mag covering all sorts of electronic music and New Wave.

So I found a few penpals from East Germany pretty quickly (their hunger for new contacts and new experiences was quite palpable!) and of course, all of my penpals were also DM fans! You need something to write about, right? And back then the only things I would write about other than Depeche Mode were Front 242, Nitzer Ebb, and Skinny Puppy.

In spring 1990 it was about time to see East Germany myself instead of just reading about it. So I followed the invitation of a guy from Dresden, with whom the exchange of letters was particularly diligent and who also ran a local fan club, to come over and attend with him a Depeche Mode convention in nearby Meißen, on the doorsteps of Dresden.

After a long train ride, and the weird experience of the infamously smelly wagons of the East German Reichsbahn, I arrived in Dresden, and in a completely different world which almost felt like another planet! Dresden is certainly a beautiful city but many houses were just down-and-out and in a pitiful state after decades of neglect and lack of investment.

The whole city felt grey to me as there were no neon lights, no outdoor advertising, no colourful shops and bars trying to attract customers. Just the grey reality of a socialist state! I actually liked it.

My pen pal Karsten picked me up at the train station and soon I met his friends. All of them DM fans, of course! I was used to most people at my age being also fans, unless they weren't metalheads or rather into rivals U2, but in East Germany, it was a different scale!

You could write entire books about the fandom in the former GDR, and some people did, but suffice to say that being a Depeche Mode fan was a complete youth culture of its own! Like being a Punk or being part of the Goth subculture.

A particular eye-opener was when we headed to the train station on Saturday to travel to Meißen. We received the news that the Depeche Mode convention, which was planned as an open-air event, was cancelled because of the heavy rains.

As we were at the train station already we waited for the local train from Meißen to come for some trains, and when the train opened its doors it cast a mass of black-clad DM fans!

I had never seen so many DM fans outside a DM gig, and even at the band's shows, I had never before seen so many Dave- and Martin-lookalikes like on this Saturday in Dresden! Later we went to a youth club where the DJ (rather a CJ as he played cassettes!) played about 50% Depeche tunes.

I asked Karsten if it was because of the cancelled DM convention and the fact that so many DM fans were at the youth club. The simple answer was "No, it's the usual Saturday night programme here!"

Depeche Mode were really big in West Germany but it was actually no comparison to the massive fandom in the old GDR. East Germany seemed like Depeche Mode wonderland to me, and the DIY culture there was pretty awe-inspiring.

Fans over there couldn't simply go to a store to buy records or clothes to dress like their heroes, they had to improvise with the stuff they had at hand and make it all by themselves, from patches and accessories to shirts and leather jackets. And the music was traded on tapes as you couldn't buy it anywhere, except for the 'Greatest Hits' released on state-owned record label Amiga in 1987.

So there was an entire country packed with fans hungry to get their hands on anything DM related, now that the wall and strict censorship no longer kept them from Western sources. There was just one little problem: East and West were still separate nations, with different currencies! And with the 'Mark der DDR' of the ruined socialist state, you could buy fuck-all elsewhere.

The 'Währungsunion', when West Germany's Deutsche Mark was introduced to East Germany as the official currency and the first major step towards the reunification, didn't happen until July 1, 1990. Not too big a problem for your record buying plans, I guess, as you just had to be a little more patient.

But a bloody *big* problem if you want to grab the first real chance to see your favourite band live for the first time! Sure, there was the legendary DM gig in East Berlin in March 1988, but the audience was handpicked from the FDJ youth organisation and officials went to great lengths to hide the fact that DM would be playing as long as they could and masked the event like a special birthday celebration of the FDJ. The officials indeed feared riots if it was made public that DM were to play in East Berlin, and quite rightly so - there were riots!

So the 'World Violation Tour' was the first actual chance for any East German fan to see the Mode live. The problem was that the presales started in spring, months ahead of the Währungsunion, and as you might guess all dates were sold out in no time! No chance for folks who had only Mark der DDR in their wallets...

When Depeche's tour finally came to Germany in the autumn of 1990, the black market simply exploded as many, many fans from East Germany came anyway to see if they could get a ticket. No matter if it was in Hannover, Frankfurt, Hamburg or Dortmund, you always saw masses of East German fans in front of the venue. Some with happy faces as they could get hold of a ticket, some still looking for one.

Prices went sky-high, easily five or six times face value and often even more, and if you dared to hold up a ticket in front of the arena you would find yourself in a knot of people, each and everyone trying to outbid the others. There was a sense of hysteria in the air, and this surely translated to the gigs - as if they weren't hysterical enough already!

So the eleven months of the German reunification, from the Fall of the Wall in November 1989 to the actual reunion in October 1990, were all the more exciting for German fans. Of course for those from the east, in particular. 'Violator' delivered their soundtrack of the German reunion, and it is indeed interesting that the band's releases around 'Violator' marked Germany's turn of the era, like landmarks.

'Personal Jesus' was released in August 1989, stayed in the German charts for 27 weeks and was one of the big hits through autumn 1989, when the East German protests against the regime turned into a mass phenomenon. The last single off the album, 'World In My Eyes', was released on September 17 1990, shortly before the German Unity Day on October 3.

All four singles from the album, including 'Enjoy The Silence' (missing the lead in the charts by just a margin as Sinéad O'Connor's 'Nothing Compares 2 U' refused to leave the No. 1 spot) and 'Policy Of Truth', were top ten hits in Germany.

David Hasselhoff will probably cry tears of disappointment but Depeche Mode were pretty much the 'fall of the wall' act for many Germans, rather than the former 'Baywatch' star. His performance at the wall was nothing more than a publicity stunt and took place months after the actual fall of the wall – on New Year's Eve, to be precise. And some people were actually throwing stuff at him!

The Hoff, however, lends himself much more to a running gag than Depeche, so we Germans love to fuel the urban myth that The Hoff brought down the wall all by himself by singing 'Looking For Freedom'. Apparently, he started to believe the myth himself at some point.

Chapter 8

Waiting For The Night (To Fall In)

"When the four members of the band were still together, 'Violator' *was the pinnacle of us having fun."*

***

Tucked away within the vast, mostly unofficial library of Depeche Mode videos hosted on YouTube is a clip of the band that is now well-known to the loyal and fanatical fan base.

Credited to Alan Wilder and Andy Franks as the two mischief-makers who recorded the footage, Depeche Mode are captured at the MTV Video Music Awards in September 1988.

Elsewhere on the internet is a slickly produced clip of the band performing 'Strangelove' at the event in Los Angeles, but Franks and Wilder's rough and ready video montage is much more revealing and, indeed, entertaining.

The 31 minutes of camcorder footage shows the band, tour manager Franks, friend and assistant Daryl Bamonte and others getting ready for the gig at their hotel.

They are then hanging about in and around their caravan / dressing room in the ceremony venue's parking lot, essentially just waiting for a rehearsal and then the show to start.

Surrounded by the current crop of stars of the American music scene and plenty of freely available liquid refreshment, what would any group of young, successful British lads and their entourage do?

Play cricket - the band and crew had been involved in a few matches against support act Orchestral Manoeuvres In The

Dark during the 'Music For The Masses Tour', so this was not unusual – drink some more, wind each other up a lot, take the piss out of everything.

When now-manager Jonathan Kessler - provider of the infamous "A lot of money" scene when counting the merchandise and ticket receipts at the Rose Bowl in the '101' movie – arrives in a limousine, one of the band shouts "Wanker" across the parking lot, much to everyone's amusement.

The clip also shows the band being interviewed by the media and then sitting in the crowd, during the ceremony itself, watching on with mild bemusement as the Fat Boys & Chubby Checker perform on stage.

The video is a wonderful snapshot in time, with the band looking relaxed, enjoying each other's company and seemingly without a care in the world. They had achieved the unthinkable a few months before, selling out the Rose Bowl and knowing there was a movie coming via director D. A. Pennebaker in six months' time that reflected that achievement.

The camaraderie, bond and banter between the band members and the others who came along for the day – including Gahan's later wife and former US press officer Teresa Conroy – are palpable. This, at least outwardly, was a happy time for the nine-year-old band.

By all accounts, Depeche Mode managed to enjoy and maintain the upbeat vibe through the first few months of recording 'Violator', in Milan from May 1989, where the band, Flood, Bamonte and studio assistants would regularly visit the city's bars and clubs.

The secluded Puk studio in Denmark did not lend itself to lots of partying but the creative process and what was emerging from the sessions seemed to ensure that a positive atmosphere remained.

It would be a further five months before the merry-go-round of activity for the promotion of 'Enjoy The Silence' and 'Violator' itself kicked in – a process that the band historically didn't particularly enjoy.

But yet again, despite the relentless schedule of press interviews, photo and video shoots, album signings and rehearsals for the forthcoming tour in the spring of 1990, this was an extremely good time to be in the Depeche Mode camp.

***

By the end of the 'World Violation Tour', Depeche Mode had reached new heights that most people, perhaps even the band themselves, did not foresee.

In nine years, they had gone from smiling synthpop boys to the biggest band in the world. Their climb to that peak had been steady and almost unnoticed until 'Violator' changed everything.

If the band wanted to continue succeeding and growing at a rate of their choosing, 'Violator' ensured that Depeche Mode had little choice as to how successful they were going to be.

The album was embraced by millions of people, the singles lodged in top tens worldwide and the concerts sold out faster than Depeche Mode concerts had ever done before.

Depeche Mode were in new territory – all of a sudden, they had moved onto a new plane.

The 'World Violation Tour' was a tour that mixed hedonism with standout performances. The band were of course no strangers to enjoying a party after a concert, but the 'World Violation Tour' saw the partying hit new levels. It is easy to see why. The band were on a crest of a wave and deservedly enjoying the well-earned trappings of success.

The conclusion of the tour brought to an end a decade of near-constant work for the band. They had followed a well-worn path of releasing an album, touring, resting briefly, releasing an album, touring and so on from 'Speak & Spell' to 'Violator', during which time they had lost a key member, gained another, reimagined their sound with each album and gradually become a must-see live act. That relentless schedule allied to a relentless partying schedule was bound to take a toll.

For the first time in their career, the band took a prolonged period off following the end of 'World Violation'. They needed time to recharge their batteries, take stock and plan their next move. While Depeche Mode now tend to operate on a cycle of an album every four years, the three-year gap between 'Violator' and 'Songs Of Faith And Devotion' was unheard of at the time.

After a nine-month-long party, readjusting to normal life, a life where you must cope with day-to-day mundanities such as ordering or making your own food must be extremely difficult. You are a world-famous musician who has spent the best part of a year hearing and being told just how great you and your band are, and then there is silence.

The band stayed true to their word in 1991. They won the Brit Award for Best Single at that year's Brit Awards but sent BBC Radio 1 DJ Simon Mayo to collect the award on their behalf.

They were asked to contribute a new song to the soundtrack of a new Wim Wenders film ('Until The End Of The World') and they duly obliged with 'Death's Door'. The song was recorded by Martin and Alan. Dave, by that stage resident in America, did not want to travel back to England to record the vocals, so Martin provided them.

The soundtrack album was released in the latter part of 1991 and the Jazz Mix version of the song was sent to fan club members in 1992 on a flexidisc given away with issue 16 of 'Bong', the Depeche Mode fan club magazine.

In terms of band output, that is all there was until 'I Feel You' was released in February 1993.

The expectations that greeted the announcement of a new Depeche Mode album were sky-high. The band had redefined electronic music with 'Violator' and their next move was keenly anticipated. Since 'Violator's release, electronic music had changed dramatically.

The late 1980s acid house movement had blossomed into the rave scene in the band's home country with innovative acts such as LFO and Orbital taking the Depeche Mode blueprint and reinventing it.

In the US, electronic music tended towards a more aggressive, industrial feel, pioneered by Nine Inch Nails, whose 'Pretty Hate Machine' album was deeply influenced by 'Black

Celebration' and Mute. The album was partly recorded with John Fryer at Blackwing, where Depeche recorded their first albums.

Ambient electronics came to the fore for a spell with The Orb channelling a prog feel through an electronic template redolent of Depeche Mode's more experimental 12-inch remixes. Everywhere you looked, bands and genres popped up, each unique but each influenced in some way by Depeche Mode.

Their work and the success it attained showed what was possible and indicated what electronic music could do. Gone was the idea that electronic music meant cold, emotionless music with no depth.

Depeche Mode had disabused the world of that notion with 'Violator' and the myriad of bands it influenced and encouraged leapt on its success, using it as a springboard for their own, in many cases, distinctly un-Depeche Mode-like releases.

How then would the forefathers of this vast mix of genres, sounds and approaches to recording respond with their next album? How could they build on 'Violator's sound and success, and take a further leap forward?

Releasing 'Violator Part Two' would have been a mistake but that was never going to happen. Depeche Mode had always moved on with each new release, pushing themselves and challenging their audience.

Their next release, the distinctly un-'Violator'-like 'Songs Of Faith And Devotion', did just that. From the moment fans saw pictures of a newly bearded and long-haired Dave in 'Bong' magazine, sitting astride a motorcycle in his new Los Angeles home, it was clear the band were going to be a different proposition when they returned.

When 'I Feel You' was released, the sense of shock throughout the music world as a whole, never mind the Depeche Mode part of that, was seismic. What on earth had happened to Depeche Mode?

The well-told tale of 'Songs Of Faith And Devotion' and the issues each band member faced on the subsequent fourteen-month tour is a tale for another book. Suffice to say that the levels of partying the band had reached on 'World Violation' continued during the 'Devotional', 'Exotic' and 'USA94' tours, arguably even reaching new levels as they progressed.

Depeche Mode dealt with the expectations that 'Violator' and 'World Violation' created head-on with 'Songs Of Faith And Devotion'. The party carried on, the successes and sold-out concerts kept coming and, again, the band seemed unstoppable.

But that's the trouble with prolonged partying. It eventually has to stop and when it does, you pay a price for it.

By the end of the 'Songs Of Faith And Devotion' tour, the band were in a mess. Dave had his by-now well-known issues, Fletcher had taken the last part of the tour off to get help for mental health issues, Gore was becoming reliant on alcohol and Wilder was fed up.

The contrast between the two eras couldn't be starker.

But the issues within the band surfaced long before the notorious partying on the tour began, with the Madrid recording session in 1992 deemed a "fucking waste of time" by Wilder, according to Flood.

Tensions between band members were not unusual but this time there appeared to be little desire or ability to resolve them. Depeche Mode were in new, rather grown-up territory that featured a toxic mix of stubbornness, drugs, lots of pressure to match the success of 'Violator' and creative differences.

The dark and brooding 'Songs Of Faith And Devotion', while lapped up by fans and critics as another daring new move by Depeche Mode to expand their sound and what people expected of them, was a macro indicator of deeper issues.

As Flood later noted, 'Violator' and 'Songs Of Faith And Devotion' were exact tributes to capturing the "emotions of the time and the chemistry between the people".

A consequence of the problems that emerged during the recording of 'Songs Of Faith And Devotion' was the fate of Wilder's membership in Depeche Mode.

He felt he was not receiving the recognition that he deserved for his role in the band and was unhappy at deteriorating relations between himself and unnamed band members. As a result, on June 1 1995, his 36th birthday, Wilder announced that he was leaving Depeche Mode.

The post-partying hangover had kicked in for Depeche Mode. The man partly responsible for framing the sound that had propelled them to their status as one of the world's biggest bands had gone and it seemed that history was repeating itself.

Once again, Depeche Mode had been reduced to a trio and, once again, people were genuinely questioning whether or not the band could carry on. As sessions for 'Ultra' commenced, Dave was in very bad shape and Martin wondered if the next release he would be involved in would be a Gore solo effort. They pulled through of course and 'Ultra', the ultimate hangover album, was released in 1997 to much-justified praise.

The circumstances that led to Wilder's departure and the band's general state were not solely the fault of 'Songs Of Faith And Devotion'. 'Violator' and 'World Violation' were their genesis.

Without that huge success, it is highly unlikely that 'Songs Of Faith And Devotion' would have been made. What Depeche Mode would have sounded like had 'Violator' not been the success it was is a moot point of course, but they would certainly not have taken the bold approach that 'Songs Of Faith And Devotion' took.

Without 'Violator', Depeche Mode would not be the band they currently are, a band that has survived numerous setbacks but one that has remained at the very top, especially when it comes to live performance. Their resilience in the face of adversity is one of their key strengths, their determination an apparent factor from day one of their existence.

The night fell in on Depeche Mode post-'Violator', but not for five years. They held themselves together long enough to push the boundaries once again in 1993 and 1994, but even a band this resolute, this tough, couldn't keep that up indefinitely.

It is to their credit that they dealt with the blows that landed, survived and continue to survive to this day.

It is true to say that if 'Violator' had not succeeded in the way it did, Depeche Mode would be a very different proposition indeed. It is also true to say that we are all lucky they succeeded and that they kept on succeeding, even when it seemed they were doomed to fail.

Appendix

Timeline Of An Era

Date	Location	Activity
Saturday, June 18, 1988	Pasadena Rose Bowl, Pasadena, USA	Gig (last show of the 'Music For The Masses Tour')
Sunday, June 19, 1988	Mojave Desert and Little Rock, USA	Photo shoot - Anton Corbijn, Dave Gahan, Martin Gore, Andy Fletcher
Monday, June 20, 1988	Mojave Desert, USA	Photo shoot - Anton Corbijn and Alan Wilder
August 1988	Swanyard Studios, London, UK	Mastering '101'
September 1988	Senate House, London, UK	'Strangelove 88' video shoot - director Martyn Atkins, Dave Gahan, Martin, Andy Fletcher and Alan Wilder
Wednesday, September 7, 1988	Universal Amphitheater, Los Angeles, USA	MTV Video Awards - Dave Gahan, Martin Gore, Andy Fletcher and Alan Wilder
Thursday, September 29, 1988	Prague, Czech Republic	Three-day photo shoot - Anton Corbijn, Dave Gahan, Martin Gore, Andy Fletcher and Alan Wilder
Friday, December 09, 1988	New York, USA	'101' draft screening - DA Pennebaker, Dave Gahan, Martin Gore, Andy Fletcher and Alan Wilder
December 1988	London, UK	Photo shoot - Anton Corbijn, Dave Gahan, Martin Gore, Andy Fletcher and Alan Wilder
Monday, February 13, 1989	Worldwide	Single release for 'Everything Counts (Live)'
Wednesday, February 22, 1989	Dominion Theatre, London, UK	Premiere '101' movie

Date	Location	Activity
Saturday, February 25, 1989	San Remo Festival, Italy	TV performance - 'Everything Counts (Live)'
February 1989	London, UK	Filming for BBC2 documentary 'The Story Of 101'
February 1989	London, UK	Photo shoot - Kevin Davies, Dave Gahan, Martin Gore, Andy Fletcher and Alan Wilder
Monday, March 13, 1989	Worldwide	Album release for '101'
May 1989	Logic Studios, Milan, Italy	Recording sessions for 'Violator'
May 1989	Milan, Italy	Photo shoot - Anton Corbijn, Dave Gahan, Martin Gore, Andy Fletcher and Alan Wilder
June 1989	Tabernas Desert, Almeria, Spain	Video shoot for 'Personal Jesus' - Anton Corbijn, Dave Gahan, Martin Gore, Andy Fletcher and Alan Wilder
Monday, June 12, 1989	Worldwide	EP release for Martin Gore solo project 'Counterfeit'
June 1989	Puk Studio, Randers, Denmark	Recording sessions for 'Violator'
August 1989	Puk Studio, Randers, Denmark	Photo shoot - Anton Corbijn, Dave Gahan, Martin Gore, Andy Fletcher and Alan Wilder
Tuesday, August 29, 1989	Worldwide	Single release for 'Personal Jesus'
Sept 1989	The Church Studios, London, UK	Recording sessions for 'Violator'
Friday, October 13, 1989	London, UK	Photo shoot - Midori Tsukagoshi, Dave Gahan, Martin Gore, Andy Fletcher and Alan Wilder

Date	Location	Activity
Friday, October 13, 1989	London, UK	TV performance - 'Personal Jesus'
Tuesday, November 28, 1989	London, UK	Video shoot for 'Enjoy The Silence' - Anton Corbijn, Dave Gahan, Martin Gore, Andy Fletcher and Alan Wilder
Dec 1989	Balmoral, Scotland, UK	Video shoot for 'Enjoy The Silence' - Anton Corbijn and Dave Gahan
Jan 1990	London, UK	Photo shoot - Claude Gassian, Dave Gahan, Martin Gore, Andy Fletcher and Alan Wilder
Jan 1990	Alvor, Portugal	Video shoot for 'Enjoy The Silence' - Anton Corbijn and Dave Gahan
Jan 1990	Swiss Alps, Switzerland	Video shoot for 'Enjoy The Silence' - Anton Corbijn and Dave Gahan
Monday, January 15, 1990	London, UK	Photo shoot - Kevin Westenberg, Dave Gahan, Martin Gore, Andy Fletcher and Alan Wilder
Feb 1990	London, UK	Photo shoot - AJ Barratt, Dave Gahan, Martin Gore, Andy Fletcher and Alan Wilder
Monday, February 05, 1990	Worldwide	Single release for 'Enjoy The Silence'
Monday, February 26, 1990	Worldwide	Single release for 'Enjoy The Silence (Quad Final Mix)'

Date	Location	Activity
March 1990	Diner, New York City, USA	Photo shoot - Anton Corbijn, Dave Gahan, Martin Gore, Andy Fletcher and Alan Wilder
March 1990	Meatpacking District, New York City, USA	Video shoot for 'Policy Of Truth' - Anton Corbijn, Dave Gahan, Martin Gore, Andy Fletcher and Alan Wilder
Saturday, March 10, 1990	New York City, USA	Three-day video shoot for 'World Violation Tour' visuals - Anton Corbijn, Dave Gahan, Martin Gore, Andy Fletcher and Alan Wilder
Monday, March 19, 1990	Worldwide	Album release for 'Violator'
Monday, March 19, 1990	Joshua Tree National Park, USA	Photo shoot - Anton Corbijn, Dave Gahan, Martin Gore, Andy Fletcher and Alan Wilder
Tuesday, March 20, 1990	The Wherehouse, Los Angeles, USA	In-store album signing
Saturday, March 24, 1990	World Trade Center, New York City, USA	Video shoot for 'Enjoy The Silence' French TV appearance - Dave Gahan, Martin Gore, Andy Fletcher and Alan Wilder
Thursday, May 03, 1990	Nomis Studios, London, UK	Seven-day rehearsal for 'World Violation Tour'
Monday, May 07, 1990	Worldwide	Single release for 'Policy Of Truth'

Date	Location	Activity
Tuesday, May 15, 1990	London, UK	Photo shoot - John Stoddart, Dave Gahan, Martin Gore, Andy Fletcher and Alan Wilder
May 1990	Pensacola, USA	Production rehearsals for 'World Violation Tour'
Monday, May 28, 1990	Pensacola Civic Center, Pensacola, USA	Gig (first show of the 'World Violation Tour')
Wednesday, May 30, 1990	Orlando Arena, Orlando, USA	Gig
Thursday, May 31, 1990	Miami Arena, Miami, USA	Gig
Saturday, June 02, 1990	Sun Dome, Tampa, USA	Gig
Monday, June 04, 1990	Lakewood Amphitheater, Atlanta, USA	Gig
Wednesday, June 06, 1990	Merriweather Post Pavilion, Columbia, USA	Gig
Friday, June 08, 1990	Saratoga Performing Arts Center, Saratoga, USA	Gig
Saturday, June 09, 1990	Great Woods Center, Mansfield, USA	Gig
Sunday, June 10, 1990	Great Woods Center, Mansfield, USA	Gig
June 1990	New York City, USA	Photo shoot - Anton Corbijn, Dave Gahan, Martin Gore, Andy Fletcher and Alan Wilder

Date	Location	Activity
Wednesday, June 13, 1990	Spectrum, Philadelphia, USA	Gig
Thursday, June 14, 1990	Spectrum, Philadelphia, USA	Gig
Saturday, June 16, 1990	Giants Stadium, East Rutherford, USA	Gig
Monday, June 18, 1990	New York City, USA	Photo shoot - Elsa Trillat, Dave Gahan, Martin Gore, Andy Fletcher and Alan Wilder
Monday, June 18, 1990	Radio City Music Hall, New York City, USA	Gig
Wednesday, June 20, 1990	Civic Center, Ottawa, Canada	Gig (cancelled)
Thursday, June 21, 1990	Forum, Montreal, Canada	Gig
Friday, June 22, 1990	CNE Grandstand, Toronto, Canada	Gig
Sunday, June 24, 1990	Coca-Cola Star Lake Amphitheater, Pittsburgh, USA	Gig
Monday, June 25, 1990	Riverbend Music Center, Cincinnati, USA	Gig
Tuesday, June 26, 1990	Blossom Music Center, Cleveland, USA	Gig
Thursday, June 28, 1990	Pine Knob Music Theater, Clarkston, USA	Gig
Friday, June 29, 1990	Pine Knob Music Theater, Clarkston, USA	Gig

Date	Location	Activity
Saturday, June 30, 1990	Marcus Amphitheater, Milwaukee, USA	Gig
Monday, July 02, 1990	World Music Theater, Chicago, USA	Gig
Tuesday, July 03, 1990	World Music Theater, Chicago, USA	Gig
Thursday, July 05, 1990	Cynthis Woods Mitchell Pavilion, Houston, USA	Gig
Friday, July 06, 1990	Cynthis Woods Mitchell Pavilion, Houston, USA	Gig
Sunday, July 08, 1990	Starplex Amphitheater, Dallas, USA	Gig
Monday, July 09, 1990	Starplex Amphitheater, Dallas, USA	Gig
Wednesday, July 11, 1990	Red Rocks Amphitheater, Denver, USA	Gig
Thursday, July 12, 1990	Red Rocks Amphitheater, Denver, USA	Gig
Saturday, July 14, 1990	Olympic Saddledone, Calgary, Canada	Gig
Monday, July 16, 1990	Pacific Coliseum, Canada	Gig
Wednesday, July 18, 1990	Memorial Coliseum, Portland, USA	Gig

Date	Location	Activity
Friday, July 20, 1990	Shoreline Amphitheater, Mountain View, USA	Gig
Saturday, July 21, 1990	Shoreline Amphitheater, Mountain View, USA	Gig
Sunday, July 22, 1990	California Exposition & State Fair, Sacramento, USA	Gig
Tuesday, July 24, 1990	Park West Amphitheater, Salt Lake City, USA	Gig (cancelled)
Wednesday, July 25, 1990	Salt Palace, Salt Lake City, USA	Gig
Thursday, July 26, 1990	Motor Vu Theater, Tooele, USA	Video shoot for 'World In My Eyes' - Anton Corbijn, Dave Gahan, Martin Gore, Andy Fletcher and Alan Wilder
Friday, July 27, 1990	Veterans Memorial Coliseum, Phoenix, USA	Gig
Saturday, July 28, 1990	San Diego Sports Arena, San Diego, USA	Gig
Sunday, July 29, 1990	San Diego Sports Arena, San Diego, USA	Gig
Tuesday, July 31, 1990	Los Angeles, USA	Video shoot for 'Clean' - Anton Corbijn and Martin Gore

Date	Location	Activity
Tuesday, July 31, 1990	San Diego Sports Arena, San Diego, USA	Gig
Wednesday, August 01, 1990	Universal Ampitheater, Universal City, USA	Gig
Thursday, August 02, 1990	Los Angeles, USA	Video shoot for 'Halo' - Anton Corbijn and Martin Gore
Saturday, August 04, 1990	Dodger Stadium, Los Angeles, USA	Gig
Sunday, August 05, 1990	Dodger Stadium, Los Angeles, USA	Gig
Friday, August 31, 1990	Hordern Pavilion, Sydney, Australia	Gig
Saturday, September 01, 1990	Festival Hall, Melbourne, Australia	Gig (cancelled)
Tuesday, September 04, 1990	Shimin Kaikan Hall, Fukuoka, Japan	Gig
Thursday, September 06, 1990	World Kinen Hall, Kobe, Japan	Gig
Saturday, September 08, 1990	Ishikawa Koseinenkin Hall, Kanazawa, Japan	Gig
Sunday, September 09, 1990	Nagoya-Shi Kokaido, Nagoya, Japan	Gig
Tuesday, September 11, 1990	Nippon Budokan, Tokyo, Japan	Gig

Date	Location	Activity
Wednesday, September 12, 1990	Nippon Budokan, Tokyo, Japan	Gig
Monday, September 17, 1990	Worldwide	Single release for 'World In My Eyes'
Friday, September 28, 1990	Forest National, Brussels, Belgium	Gig
Saturday, September 29, 1990	Westfalenhallen, Dortmund, Germany	Gig
Sunday, September 30, 1990	Westfalenhallen, Dortmund, Germany	Gig
Tuesday, October 02, 1990	Valby-Hallen, Copenhagen, Denmark	Gig
Wednesday, October 03, 1990	Valby-Hallen, Copenhagen, Denmark	Gig
Friday, October 05, 1990	Scandiavium, Gothenburg, Sweden	Gig
Saturday, October 06, 1990	Globe Arena, Stockholm, Sweden	Gig
Monday, October 08, 1990	Festhalle Frankfurt, Frankfurt, Germany	Gig
Tuesday, October 09, 1990	Messehalle, Hanover, Germany	Gig

Date	Location	Activity
Thursday, October 11, 1990	Halle Tony Garnier, Lyon, France	Gig
Friday, October 12, 1990	Hallenstadion, Zurich, Switzerland	Gig
Sunday, October 14, 1990	Festhalle Frankfurt, Frankfurt, Germany	Gig
Monday, October 15, 1990	Hanns-Martin-Schleter-Halle, Stuffgart, Germany	Gig
Wednesday, October 17, 1990	Olympiahalle, Munich, Germany	Gig
Friday, October 19, 1990	Palais Omnisports Bercy, Paris, France	Gig (cancelled)
Sunday, October 21, 1990	Palais Omnisports Bercy, Paris, France	Gig
Monday, October 22, 1990	Palais Omnisports Bercy, Paris, France	Gig
Tuesday, October 23, 1990	Palais Omnisports Bercy, Paris, France	Gig
Thursday, October 25, 1990	Stade Couvert Regional, Lievin, France	Gig
Friday, October 26, 1990	Ahoy Rotterdam, Rotterdam, The Netherlands	Gig

Date	Location	Activity
Sunday, October 28, 1990	Alsterdorfer Sporthalle, Hamburg, Germany	Gig
Monday, October 29, 1990	Alsterdorfer Sporthalle, Hamburg, Germany	Gig
Wednesday, October 31, 1990	Deutschlandhalle, Hamburg, Germany	Gig
Thursday, November 01, 1990	Deutschlandhalle, Hamburg, Germany	Gig
Saturday, November 03, 1990	Rhenus Sport, Stasbourg, France	Gig
Monday, November 05, 1990	Worldwide	Book release for 'Strangers'
Monday, November 05, 1990	Palau Sant Jordi, Barcelona, Spain	Gig
Tuesday, November 06, 1990	Worldwide	Video release for 'Strange Too'
Wednesday, November 07, 1990	Palacio de Deportes, Madrid, Spain	Gig
Friday, November 09, 1990	Palais des Sports, Marseille, France	Gig
Sunday, November 11, 1990	Palatrussardi, Milan, Italy	Gig

Date	Location	Activity
Monday, November 12, 1990	PalaEUR, Rome, Italy	Gig
Wednesday, November 14, 1990	Patinoire de Meriadeck	Gig
Thursday, November 15, 1990	Patinoire de Meriadeck	Gig
Saturday, November 17, 1990	Parc du Penfeld	Gig
Monday, November 19, 1990	Wembley Arena, London, UK	Gig
Tuesday, November 20, 1990	Wembley Arena, London, UK	Gig
Thursday, November 22, 1990	NEC, Birmingham, UK	Gig
Friday, November 23, 1990	Wembley Arena, London, UK	Gig
Monday, November 26, 1990	NEC, Birmingham, UK	Gig
Tuesday, November 27, 1990	NEC, Birmingham, UK	Gig (last show of the 'World Violation Tour')

About the authors

David McElroy became a Depeche Mode fan when growing up in Castle Douglas in Southwest Scotland. He first heard 'Enjoy The Silence' in his parents' car on a day when he was too lazy to walk to school and from that point he was hooked. David now lives in Glasgow with his increasingly out-of-control Depeche Mode collection and runs the Depeche Mode blog Almost Predictable Almost. His first Depeche Mode gig was the band's 1993 show at Crystal Palace and, in April 2017, David ran the band's Facebook page for a day as part of their Fan Takeover campaign.

Kevin May was a journalist for nearly 30 years before switching to academic studies in the area of mental health in 2022. He edited a number of publications during his journalism career, including titles covering the travel and media industries. Kevin has co-hosted five podcasts and moderated at dozens of events in the US, China, India, Australia, Singapore and across Europe. Coincidentally, an early job in journalism was as a reporter in Essex, covering Depeche Mode's hometown of Basildon. He first saw the band in 1990 on the 'World Violation Tour'.

Lightning Source UK Ltd.
Milton Keynes UK
UKHW021639051022
409954UK00013B/240

9 781803 812250